THE DOURO RIVER

Pinhão

Foz Tua

VALEIRA DAM

Foz do Sabor

Senhora
da Ribeira

POCINHO DAM

Vila Nova de Foz Côa •

**CORK BOAT
LAUNCHED HERE**

Almendra •

Barca
de Alva

S P A I N

0 *Miles*   10   20

0 *Kilometers*   20

Jeffrey L. Ward

CORK BOAT

CORK BOAT

John Pollack

PANTHEON BOOKS, NEW YORK

Library of Congress Cataloging-in-Publication Data

Pollack, John.
Cork boat / John Pollack.
p. cm.
ISBN 0-375-42257-9
1. Boats and boating—Duero River (Spain and Portugal). 2. Pollack,
John—Journeys—Portugal. 3. Cork. I. Title.

GV776.62.A2P65 2004   797.1'0949—dc21   2003054838

www.pantheonbooks.com

Book design by M. Kristen Bearse
Illustrations by Tim Purus
Map by Jeffrey L. Ward

Printed in the United States of America
First Edition
2   4   6   8   9   7   5   3   1

It wasn't, of course, the beginning, for who can say where a voyage starts—not the actual passage but the dream of a journey and its urge to find a way?

—from *River-Horse,*
by William Least Heat-Moon

CORK BOAT

A Boy and a Boat

My first boat sank. I was six years old and had hammered it together from old orange crates and split firewood, sealing the cracks with bumper stickers from an Ann Arbor City Council candidate named Ulrich Stoll. When it was finished, I walked around the neighborhood and invited people to the launch. Saturday morning, at the pond.

On the big day, my family, a few neighbors, and one or two of their dogs dutifully assembled at the small, reedy marsh at the end of our block. As my mom cinched on my life jacket, my dad set the boat in the water. More excited than nervous, I stepped aboard.

It was a short voyage—straight down. Within seconds, brown water started gurgling up around my ankles, then gushing over the sides. Before I could even think about abandoning ship, it was all over. There I stood, knee-deep in water, my boat stuck fast on the muddy bottom.

Afterward, I wheeled the boat home on my wagon and junked it behind our garage. But I wasn't discouraged. I was happy—I had built a real boat! And I was already thinking about my next one. I would just have to build it out of something guaranteed to float, no matter what.

I eventually settled on wine corks, the kind my parents pulled out of the bottle at the dinner table once or twice a week. Since it was impossible to sink a cork, I reasoned, it would be even more impossible to sink a lot of corks.

And so I started saving them, one by one.

From then on, all my parents' corks went into a wooden bowl on the kitchen counter. To them, whether or not I could ever save enough corks was irrelevant. In our family, imagination itself was a prime virtue, and they encouraged my older sister, Sara, and me to let ours run free. In a home governed largely by expectations, not rules, I can remember only one explicit mandate from my mom: we weren't allowed to get bored. Sara and I—separated by only a year and a half—were united by that challenge, and we constantly conspired to keep things interesting.

My parents set a good example. My mom was always busy in those early years, teaching dance and running local political campaigns. Apart from the surplus bumper stickers we often got as a result, Sara and I also learned that hard-fought battles, even losing ones, were worth the effort. In 1972, the two of us organized a dozen neighborhood kids to hold a bake sale for George McGovern, pulling an assortment of cupcakes and cookies from house to house on our wagons. I recall hauling them up one especially steep driveway, a veritable Everest, and ringing the doorbell at its summit. I can still see the owner, in a dark blue dress and towering bouffant, answering our pitch with a friendly but firm "I'm sorry. We're for Mr. Nixon."

My dad was a popular professor of geophysics at the University of Michigan, where he still teaches today. Always eager to travel the world, he saw no need to choose between family and fieldwork. So wherever he went, we went, too, whether it meant flying into the Amazon on a rattletrap Cessna, plying the waters of Lake Titicaca in a traditional reed boat, or jouncing down some of the worst roads in Africa in a mud-spattered Land Rover.

If our family travels weren't always comfortable or easy, they were never dull. In Zambia, we once picked up a tall hitchhiker in a red jumpsuit who carried a nine-foot spear. He smelled terrible, and Sara and I, sharing the backseat with him, secretly held our breath for as long as possible. Another time, when we were camping on an uninhabited island in Africa's Lake Tanganyika, Sara spotted a cobra slithering toward our open tent. Within seconds, my mom grabbed a nearby shovel and, swinging it like a machete, chopped off the snake's head.

Later that same year, as we were crossing the Zambezi River from Zambia to Botswana on a small, jury-rigged ferry, a patrol boat from Rhodesia roared up the river and began circling us like a shark, trying to swamp the ferry's outboard and send us drifting downstream into Rhodesian territory. Much to my dad's dismay, my mom gave the soldiers a defiant, international gesture for "kiss my ass." But we made it across safely. Sara and I assumed all of this was quite normal.

Back home in Ann Arbor, we traveled just as widely in our minds, reading book after book about explorers, pioneers, and inventors who helped make history and change the world. In our basement, Sara and I transformed an old refrigerator box into a spaceship, where we spent many happy hours exploring strange planets in faraway galaxies. I even sacrificed a few corks—the kind with plastic tops—for the cause. Inserted through the cardboard walls of our spacecraft, they made excellent knobs for adjusting the booster rockets.

When I was eleven, we moved to England for a year, for one of my dad's sabbaticals. We lived in Durham, a small northern cathedral town, in a four-hundred-year-old gatekeeper's cottage overlooking the River Wear. Every morning, Sara and I would put on our school uniforms and trudge off to the Durham Johnston Grammar Technical School, a gray, Dickensian institution where teachers—or "masters," as they were called—required us to stand at attention whenever they entered the room, and complete our lessons with fountain pens.

But if the stern traditionalists at Durham Johnston were

inclined to view Sara and me as wayward, latter-day colonials, we took it upon ourselves to excel to such a degree that there would be little doubt that the "Yanks," as we were known, had not only won the Revolution but were first in their class, too.

And then, in a few horrible moments, my whole life changed. Leaving England, we took a family trip to India. After sharing a fun week aboard a houseboat on a gorgeous lake in Kashmir, my parents hired guides to take us all pony-trekking up into the Himalayas. Crossing a swollen river, Sara's pony slipped on a rock and threw her into the rushing waters. My dad and two of our guides sprinted in to save her, but the thundering rapids and boulders overwhelmed them. Sara, along with one of the men who tried to save her, hit the rocks and was swept away. We searched the river for two days as we hiked out, but never found them. She was fourteen.

I was devastated beyond comprehension. Sara had been my best friend, and in a single, terrible fluke—just a few yards from safety—she had been taken from me forever. Gone were the games, the laughter, the mischievous conspiracies of our childhood. And gone were any illusions that the world was safe, that parents were all-powerful, or that life was fun. I might still have been a kid, but my childhood was over.

Already a close family, we pulled together even more. Still, the years of adolescence that followed were an exercise in abject misery, and I struggled through by channeling my grief into a frenetic schedule of study, sports, and music lessons.

One of the few bright spots in junior high was building a raft with my best friend, Andrew, out of 126 cardboard milk cartons and several rolls of duct tape.

About ten feet long, the boat featured a sweeping prow that resembled a Viking ship, complete with a dragon's head whose pointed horns were half-pint cartons, emptied of their half-and-half. We called our vessel the SS *Milky Way*, and launched it in the Huron River to a smattering of applause from friends and family. It floated beautifully, and we gave rides all afternoon before bringing it back to Andrew's house. Unfortunately, only a day or so later, our craft began assuming the look and the smell of blue cheese. Only reluctantly, and at the strong insistence of Andrew's dad, did we haul it to the curb for the garbageman.

Some years later, after high school, I took a summer job as a hotel groundskeeper on Mackinac Island, a small, historic resort island in Michigan's Straits of Mackinac, at the confluence of Lakes Michigan and Huron. I had first visited the island in third grade, and was fascinated by its old colonial fort and the fact that it banned cars altogether. If you wanted to get around on Mackinac you either walked, rode your bicycle, or climbed aboard a horse-drawn wagon. More than anything, I loved all the boats that jammed its harbor, and went there hoping to spend time on the water.

Seeing I was young and fit, the head groundskeeper assigned me the task of moving rocks, work that made the prospect of two months on Mackinac seem more like a sentence on

Alcatraz. After two days at hard labor, I hatched a plan. I had brought along my violin, and convinced the resort's owner to give me a tryout as a violinist in his restaurant. "I've played the violin since I was four," I said, concealing my nervousness. "I can do more for you making music than I can moving rocks."

Something of a wheeler-dealer himself, he admired my chutzpah; he also liked the idea of replacing his maître d's George Winston tapes with some live entertainment. So, for the next few days, I moved rocks by day and played violin by night. Then, when I complained that my hands could only manage one or the other, the owner shifted me to musical work altogether, and I traded my grubby jeans for a black suit, bow tie, and the easy life of a solo, strolling violinist.

The head groundskeeper grumbled at my escape from his rock pile, but I didn't care. My quarry had now become all those romantic couples who tipped so generously for a few songs at tableside.

When I was done for the night, I'd walk home and pull the crumpled bills from my pockets—along with that night's haul of corks. Not that I had plans to build the boat of my dreams anytime soon, but saving those corks reminded me, somehow, of happier times. By summer's end, when I shipped off the island, I had several hundred.

The next summer, after my freshman year at Stanford, I returned to Mackinac in style, bringing my family's sailboat, a thirteen-foot dinghy called the *Cyclone*. Rather than spend all my tip money on one of the expensive slips at the marina, I chained two cement-filled buckets together, dropped them in the middle of the harbor, and ran a heavy rope all the way up to a grease-jug float on the surface. This functional and economical mooring enabled me to keep the *Cyclone* safely out in the harbor, bobbing amid yachts four and five times its size. The only drawback to this location was that I had to swim out and back every time I wanted to go for a sail—an invigoratingly cold prospect, even in August.

The sailing, though, was worth that arctic swim. Situated in big water, Mackinac gets big wind—big enough to have sunk dozens of ships on nearby shoals. Mindful of any change in weather, I'd cinch my life jacket tight and head out of the harbor, heeling hard and dodging the giant ore freighters that barreled past on their way to and from the iron ports of Lake Superior.

I insisted on pushing the boat to its limits, and capsized more than once. But with such a little boat, I could right it fairly easily. Wearing a life jacket and my favorite sailing gloves, I felt invincible, big water or not.

Sometimes, if a friend was willing to swim for the mooring, I would sail us both over to Round Island, just across the channel. Round Island was an uninhabited, forested state park with a sandy cove, a crumbling lighthouse, and—during the hot days of July—sweet, wild raspberries growing near the beach. Even amid the swirling angst of those late adolescent years, the afternoons I spent on Round Island were the epitome of carefree summertime bliss. I swam, sunned, and ate berries until my fingers ran red, just, I imagined, like Huck Finn.

At college out in Palo Alto, between academics and work at the *Stanford Daily,* I taught sailing and built another boat. I entered it in a campus regatta requiring that all vessels be built of cardboard. Mine, resembling a crocodile, took second place.

After graduating, I spent ten years bumping between political campaigns and journalism, including a three-year stint in Spain as a freelance foreign correspondent. I even tried my hand at bullfighting once, in a village near Madrid, and lost. Though bruised and bloodied in this foolish, self-imposed test of manhood, I escaped serious injury and ended up selling a first-person account to the *Los Angeles Times* for $500, enough to pay a month's rent. Although I am not certain about it, I suspect that my opponent—despite besting me in the ring—went on to a brief, tough career in the meat business.

But no matter where I lived or what I was doing throughout that decade after college, I could never shake the nagging worry that somehow, for some reason, the well of adventure would dry up, and that my life would suddenly become boring. So I stretched out my peregrinations, year after year, determined to postpone traditional responsibilities and the trappings of adulthood as long as possible.

OVER THE HILL

At the age of thirty-three, however, I finally had to concede that I was, without a doubt, an adult. I lived in Washington, D.C., and wore a suit and tie to work. I had a retirement account. I even carried life insurance. But despite all that, I was still saving corks for the boat. I wasn't any closer to building it, really, but I hadn't given up on the idea. Even as an adult—in fact, especially as an adult—the notion of building a cork boat was just too playful, too whimsical to drop. And, in my workaday world on Capitol Hill, play and whimsy were in decidedly short supply.

I worked as a speechwriter for Congressman David Bonior of Michigan, the Democratic Whip in the U.S. House of Representatives. From a professional standpoint, my job was a good one. I shared Bonior's political values, and as his speechwriter, I had an office in the Capitol, free run of the House floor, and an inside—albeit minor—role in shaping the national political debate.

From a personal standpoint, however, the rancorous rhetorical battles with Newt Gingrich and his GOP partisans began to take their toll on me. It often seemed that we were fighting over the same stretch of muddy ground, issue after issue, vote after vote, month after month, year after year. While some of my fellow staffers relished the fight, these endless conflicts came to remind me of trench warfare in the First World War—costly, bloody, and ultimately futile.

The political stalemate found its ultimate expression in the 1998 impeachment of President Clinton. As the Congress set aside virtually all other business to investigate and prosecute Presidential blow jobs, Washington—at its best only a Gomorrah of hope—sank even further into the quagmire of hubris and hypocrisy.

Penning floor speeches for Bonior, I was in the thick of the fight. Not to defend President Clinton's opaque, self-destructive evasions about Monica Lewinsky, but to prevent the Republicans—frustrated in their legislative ambitions—from treating the Constitution like so much political toilet paper.

This epic political battle was at once fascinating, exciting, demoralizing, and exhausting. On the morning of the House impeachment vote, I took a few moments to relax at my desk—as much as that was possible with the Capitol a zoo, hundreds of protesters yelling outside my window, and a President of the United States about to be put on trial for the second time in history. By then, Bonior's speech was written and ready for delivery; I had stayed up late writing, and we had made the final edits together, in the morning.

Suddenly, the door of my office flew open and Bonior's press secretary shouted, "Livingston is resigning!" I grabbed the remote and upped the volume on my TV. Bob Livingston was the Republican Speaker-elect, and his decision was a stunning development, even on this most surreal of days.

Having already admitted to "numerous affairs" only thirty-six hours earlier, Livingston was now apparently making the best of an awkward situation. While passing up the chance to lead the House as Speaker, he said he would continue to serve in Congress for another six months as a "back-bencher," giving the governor of his state time to call a special election (and, coincidentally, giving any GOP nominee ample time to mount a strong campaign). Now, on the floor of the House, he was calling on President Clinton to resign as well—immediately.

The catcalls ceased as Democrats and Republicans alike, momentarily stunned, watched drop-jawed the unfolding drama. My immediate reaction, by contrast, was a loud four-letter expletive that also happened to describe, albeit unintentionally, Livingston's favorite extramarital activity. Even as Livingston spoke, my phone lit up with calls. I didn't answer.

Instead, I grabbed my suit jacket and began pushing my way through the crowded hallways toward the House floor. I had to find Bonior; he was scheduled to speak in about fifteen minutes, and his speech needed a rewrite.

Every writing deadline I had ever faced, in school or journalism or politics, paled in comparison to this one, not just in its crushing immediacy, but in its consequence. As I rushed into—and then out of—an emergency meeting with Bonior, Minority Leader Dick Gephardt, and a handful of grim-faced staffers, I thought to myself: Now is not the time to choke. Now is the time to stand and deliver. And so, with Bonior's communications director standing over my shoulder and the clock ticking, I sat down at my keyboard to write a new beginning.

Within ten minutes, I was standing with other staffers at the back of the packed House floor, as Bonior, standing at an oak lectern, responded to Livingston's resignation—

"We find ourselves in a destructive cycle that is eating away at our democracy. The politics of personal smear is degrading the dignity of public office, and we must not let it continue. We must put an end to it, and the only way we will stop this vicious cycle is if we stand up and refuse to give in to it, whether it's Bill Clinton or Bob Livingston. . . ."

My heart was pounding, but the chamber was rapt. Then, as Bonior's speech began entering the more familiar territory of polished text, I exhaled in quiet relief.

"Mr. Speaker, in this building are the marble halls where Daniel Webster and Henry Clay and Abraham Lincoln debated the fate of the Union. Have we sunk so low that, in these same halls, we would allow the likes of Ken Starr, and Monica Lewinsky, and Linda Tripp to ignite the constitutional crisis of our age? . . .

"It is not too late to step back from the brink. The American People desperately want us to restore some dignity and some common sense to our politics, some sense of proportion. They want us to come together. They want us to move on. . . ."

When Bonior finished, the applause was deafening—at least from the Democratic side of the aisle. Not that it changed the course of history; the GOP succeeded in impeaching Clinton on two counts later that day. What did change that day, though, was my faith in the state of our democracy. It was going to hell, and faster than I had ever imagined.

It's not that I had arrived in Washington naïve. When I was in high school, my mom had run for the Michigan State Senate and won—the first woman elected to that body in more than a decade. In the years that followed, we talked hardball politics over dinner as if it were the weather. Throughout the course of my twenties, I had worked on too many political campaigns, local and statewide, to have any optimistic illusions about the corrupt and ailing condition of America's electoral system. In 1994, my mom's narrow defeat in her underdog bid for the U.S. Senate had hammered home to me the harsh realities of modern American politics, the limits of grassroots idealism, and the overwhelming power of big money.

I had soldiered on because politics still mattered, because I thought I could make a difference, and because we Pollacks weren't supposed to quit. But now, working in Congress was putting me to the test. It wasn't just the whole impeachment saga, the holier-than-thou hypocrisy of philanderers on both sides of the aisle, or the lynch-mob mentality that fueled it. It was really more the day-to-day pettiness of Congress and so many of its members. Although I respected Bonior and admired another handful of principled, down-to-earth legislators, they were a distinct minority in these halls. There were so many more, though, Democrats and Republicans alike, who were the very definition of mediocrity, yet had come to believe their own press releases. Although it is common habit in Washington to speak on behalf of "the American People," too many elected representatives treated those American People nearest at hand—congressional staffers—like serfs in tsarist Russia.

The worst offenders were usually those middling members who, frustrated by their inability to move up in the House leadership, had reached the apex of a political career that probably began with a fourth-grade run for student council.

"Who's in charge of this?" an obese congressman hissed at

me one morning, scanning the coffee and bagels that had been laid out for a Democratic caucus. "Why isn't there any low-fat cream cheese?"

Although I happened to be standing next to the breakfast table, cup of coffee in hand, I was responsible for sound bites, not cream cheese. I just shrugged and nodded toward the caucus chairman, who, at that moment, was speaking at the podium. The fat congressman glowered, but I refused to engage. Our little exchange lasted only a few seconds, until hunger won out over petulance. His pudgy arm darted out for a glazed donut, and he lurched off to find a seat.

That was another small thing that galled me about the Hill—the unspoken rule that staffers were to remain standing in meetings with members of Congress, even if there were extra chairs in the room. It was just one more manifestation of the Hill's caste system—the "members only" elevators, the ornate "members only" dining room—that made a mockery of the institution's democratic pretensions. It seemed that if members of Congress considered themselves public servants, a lot of them considered Hill staffers to be just plain servants.

That rankled me. Having grown up in a state senator's family, I knew the sacrifices associated with public office and respected those willing to make them. But apart from the President, I never considered elected officials to be of any higher status than doctors, dentists, mechanics, teachers, accountants, business leaders, or those of any other chosen career. Politics was just one more honorable profession among many.

Given that attitude, I suppose it was inevitable that I would eventually hit the wall in this gilded arena of ego and ambition. While I still enjoyed the friendship and camaraderie of my fellow staffers, the institution made me more cynical by the day. How many times had I seen members deliver their thundering oratory to an empty House chamber, putting on a show for the C-SPAN cameras? Worse yet were the press conferences that members held in the Radio and TV Gallery, standing in front of the shelves filled with fake books, just to lend some gravitas to their empty rhetoric. Couldn't they at least buy some real books? But even this keenest of ironies was ignored in the hubbub and hyperbole of Washington. Deep down, I knew I had to get out before the rising bile of my cynicism poisoned the last of my idealism. By the time the surreal whale of impeachment finally beached itself in the Senate, my tolerance for Capitol Hill had reached a low ebb.

So I started thinking about quitting my job. Not looking for a new one, just quitting. So what if I would be leaving a prestigious job, and casting aside my so-called success? I had done my part, and I hungered now for a real break, a creative sabbatical. I needed time to pursue anything I wanted, or nothing at all. Time to let my creative aquifer recharge, and flow in a new direction.

What counted as "success," anyway? I had begun to wonder. Several months earlier, in Baltimore, I had watched a street performer on a ten-foot unicycle: he bantered casually with the crowd while juggling a machete, a toilet plunger, and a flaming torch. He had enthralled more than two hundred people for twenty minutes. Clearly, he was following his passion, however whimsical, and in his exuberant celebration of the human spirit he did his part to make the world a better place. Why couldn't I do the same?

Building the cork boat, I reasoned, fell into that same, crazy, triumph-of-the-human-spirit category. Societal expectations aside, was building a boat any less meaningful than churning out political rhetoric that fell, all too often, on deaf ears? Maybe it was time for me to redefine success. Maybe, after half a lifetime, it was time to actually build the cork boat.

Why *not* build the boat? I had talked about it for long enough. And in its playful, goofy absurdity, a cork boat was certainly the antithesis of everything Washington. The more I considered the project, the more it seemed the perfect antidote to my cynicism. Why not let whimsy fill my sails and carry me where it would? Over a period of several weeks, the idea took root. Although I kept my decision a secret, I vowed to leave the Hill by year's end, and start the twenty-first century a free man, captain of my own ship.

Now, making the decision to build a cork boat was relatively easy. Figuring out how to build it posed a much more complex challenge. To begin with, just what would a cork boat look like? How big would it be? Would it be a riverboat or a sailboat? And how would I attach all the corks? I quickly recognized that before I could even begin to answer any of these questions, I needed to determine one critical fact: How many corks would it take to keep me afloat?

So I turned to Bruce Yoon, a friend and naval architect who lived in Washington. I briefed him on the project, then asked for his help: Could he calculate roughly how many corks it would take to float the average person—say, 160 pounds?

Bruce hedged. "I design submarine docking systems. I don't know anything about cork boats."

"You're a naval architect," I insisted. "And this is a boat."

"Sure, but . . ."

I pressed and cajoled, and promised I wouldn't hold him responsible if the boat sank. All I wanted was a number. Perhaps sensing my determination, he gave in. "It's something different," he conceded. "It'll be fun." A few days later, as I was slogging through a slow Monday afternoon at the Capitol, Bruce sent me a lengthy e-mail. "First let's take a look at the basics," he wrote. "Archimedes' principle essentially states that the weight of a floating object is equal to the weight of the water it displaces. We know that our captain of the vessel weighs 160 pounds, and the cork raft will have a nominal weight as well.

"The total weight of the man and raft must be equal to the weight of the water it displaces. And as we all know, seawater weighs approximately 64 pounds per cubic foot. Let's assign the volume of water displaced the variable X. . . ."

As I started to read Bruce's calculations, my thoughts

flashed to my seventh-grade algebra teacher, Mr. Weatherbee. An amateur boatbuilder himself, Mr. Weatherbee had once helped me solve a frustrating design problem: how to construct small Styrofoam pontoons that would enable me to launch a rubber band–powered airplane from the neighbor's swimming pool. All seventeen of my previous prototypes had failed miserably, until Mr. Weatherbee suggested I try a V-shaped hydrofoil. Newly outfitted, my little plane soared from the pool with grace—the same pool, coincidentally, in which I had originally envisioned launching the cork boat.

Reining in my wandering mind, I pressed onward through the equations Bruce had laid out, impatient for his conclusion. Factoring in the density of cork and the density of water, he determined that I would need a minimum of 2.78 cubic feet of cork, or precisely 17.84 pounds of cork, to meet my basic needs. Working from figures he had looked up on the standard density and volume of cork, Bruce arrived at some basic dimensions:

"So, it would take a cork raft 6' by 4' by 1.4" to float a 160-pound person in seawater," he wrote. "This is with the entire raft submerged or floating at the waterline. You'll need to add more to it if you plan on keeping dry. . . ."

I fired back a quick thank-you and pulled out a red pen to do my own math. Factoring the measurements of a typical 1.5-inch cylindrical cork into the dimensions of Bruce's theoretical raft, I calculated that it would have to be sixty-four corks wide and ninety-six corks long, all corks positioned vertically. So the minimum, conservative, number of corks I would need, per person, was . . . 6,144.

That was it—the magic number. Six thousand one hundred and forty-four corks. I decided I liked it; its specificity seemed to confer on my plans a certain mathematical legitimacy. If I needed 6,144 corks just to float at waterline, I'd need three or four times that to stay dry. And if I hoped to take others aboard . . . the numbers were mounting fast. Estimating conservatively, I'd have to figure on a boat of 60,000 corks.

My dad, who wasn't so keen on me quitting a good job to build a cork boat in the first place, did his own math. His calculations produced a much higher number, and he sent me an e-mail warning that "measurements on small samples have too much variability and error. A large field test will be absolutely necessary for proof-of-concept."

Don't worry, I told him. I'm not going to sink.

On my next trip to Michigan, I went up into my parents' attic, crawled under the eaves, and dragged out the duffel of corks they had been dutifully filling all these years. With high hopes, I unzipped the bag, spilled some out, and did a rough calculation. It looked like there were about 3,500—more than a quarter-century of chardonnays and sauvignons blancs. Enough to float a six-year-old boy, finally, but just a fraction of those I would now need. I scooped the corks back into the bag, and zipped it up for the trip back to Washington.

It was now absolutely clear that I'd need to launch a major collection effort. But that didn't faze me. I was an organizer, and Washington was full of bars and restaurants. The big hotels in town hosted dozens and dozens of conferences every year. And with so many people coming and going, there had to be thousands of corks floating around. All I had to do was collect them, figure out the best way to attach them, and build the thing.

Of course, it would be a whole lot easier, and more fun, with a partner. As I considered some possibilities, my thoughts focused on Garth Goldstein. Garth was the younger brother of my old high school cross-country teammate and fellow Washingtonian, Brandt. When Garth and I first met, fifteen years earlier, I was a high school junior and he was a skinny, shy sixth-grader. I didn't pay much attention to him. Six years later, when I was a campus organizer on my mom's 1988 congressional campaign, I recruited him to serve as a volunteer precinct captain on Election Day. He was enthusiastic, a glutton for work, and more competent than many volunteers twice his age.

A couple of years back, after an extended undergraduate career, Garth had moved to Washington to pursue a career in architecture. Unlike the gangly adolescent I remembered, he was now a tall, opinionated man who, like Brandt and me, still wasn't quite ready to grow up. He was still a glutton for work, though, and his unkempt reddish hair and quick, animated movements seemed to capture the energy and the enthusiasm with which he tackled everything in life. The three of us got together often, to go out for Sunday pancakes, to grill burgers at Brandt's, or—in the fall—to watch our favorite football team, the Michigan Wolverines.

Like Brandt, who had recently left a highly paid job as a corporate attorney to pursue a career as a writer, Garth chafed in the structured, workaday world and was longing to scratch his creative itch. His first job in Washington had been at a somewhat pedestrian design firm, where he had quickly grown frustrated with the assignments he was given. One was to choose the interior color scheme for a new Marriott hotel somewhere in suburban Connecticut. His color choices, tame by necessity, had to be approved by several layers of management. For this free-spirited graduate of Brown University, it felt a little stifling.

Recently, he had landed a much better job at a respected architectural firm, but, uncertain if he was ready to commit to a single career, he had begun to ask himself: Do I really want to be an architect?

I suspected that the idea of building a cork boat might hold some appeal for him, so I bounced my plans off him over dinner one night. As a kid, I explained, I had originally envisioned threading fishing line through the corks, then weaving those strands together to form a raft. In thinking about the project now, as an adult, I had shifted to a design concept that seemed more practical. I would use some sort of mesh—perhaps fishnet—to enclose the corks. My idea was to create a cork mattress, or a series of cork-filled mesh tubes that could be lashed together in the form of a Viking ship.

Almost instantly, Garth started spitting out ideas of his own. The more we talked, the more excited he got. The boat obviously appealed to his appreciation of the absurd, and the technical difficulties—chief among them, how to build a single large object from so many tiny pieces—were deliciously complex.

I was struck, perhaps, by the intensity of Garth's enthusiasm for the boat, but it didn't really surprise me in principle. I had already discovered that people either appreciated immediately that a cork boat made crazy, perfect sense, or they struggled to understand why anybody would waste his time on such a pointless project. In short, there was no middle ground; they either got the boat or they didn't. Garth got it, and to the nth degree. "You're really an architect, deep down," he said. "You really know how to live."

Coming from Garth, that was high praise. Among his many exploits, he had once organized a team that rappelled down a skyscraper to install a giant piece of guerrilla art. While still in college, he had started an adventure travel company that organized back-country hiking and rafting expeditions to the Central Asian republics of the former Soviet Union. Although our adult friendship was only just developing, I admired him for both his obvious creativity and his spirit of adventure.

"Where are you going to take the boat when it's done?" he wanted to know.

"European wine country," I answered. "Maybe France.

Can't you just see it? Stopping at villages, drinking fine wines and seducing French maidens along the way?"

I was serious about France, and only half kidding about the maidens, or perhaps, more accurately, half hopeful. I made a snap decision. "Do you want to build this cork boat together?" I asked.

Garth whooped, and we high-fived. He was in.

"If we're going to build a boat, though," he said, "let's make it big!"

"How big?" I asked, wondering just how many corks he had in mind.

"Really big," he said. "*Huge.*"

"How about this," I said. "Let's make it big enough for four people. That way, each of us can bring a date and all our gear and still keep everything dry."

It was a done deal.

As summer turned to fall, we kept talking through potential design concepts. We decided that, even if our hypothetical dates weighed less than we did, a boat of 60,000 corks might not be enough to keep us all high and dry. A hundred thousand corks sounded like a safer figure to aim for, and we could always scrap the extras. So we set that as our working goal.

For the next couple of months, it remained just that—a goal. Our day jobs got busy again, and our boat project hit the doldrums. I was okay with that, because I knew the coming year would be different. Still, when it came time for me to give notice at work in mid-October, I was a little nervous. Some colleagues cautioned me about damaging my career. Garth and some others were urging me to cut myself free. When I finally broke the news to Bonior, I didn't tell him about the boat. Instead, I mentioned some creative writing projects I was eager to spend more time on, and the prospect of some part-time work for a dot-com start-up. Though disappointed to lose me, he was very gracious about my decision and wished me well. To ease the transition, I agreed to stay on through December, writing speeches to the session's bitter end.

But even as I kept hammering away on speeches about Social Security and Medicare and the Middle East, I was anxious to launch our cork-collection effort. The biggest New Year's Eve in a thousand years was fast approaching, and that meant one thing to me: thousands upon thousands of corks popping into the midnight sky. It was time to launch the project in a big way, and we needed a flier explaining our project, fast. Garth, a talented graphic designer, said he would knock one out. Together, we would hit the new millennium with our project moving full steam ahead.

THE CORK WARS

A week before Christmas, Garth sat down at his computer to create a simple, compelling graphic—a rendering of a wine cork in a round, black field. Designed as a postcard, the flier was at once simple and bold. SAVE YOUR CORKS, it said on the front, above the cork logo. WE'RE BUILDING A BOAT. On the back, it featured the stylized silhouette of a Viking ship and a one-sentence explanation of the project. "Join us in collecting 100,000 wine & champagne corks to build the world's first cork boat. You save them. We pick them up." Just in case anyone doubted our determination, we added a flip rejoinder. "Yes, we're serious."

Flier finally in hand, I ran off three hundred copies at Kinko's. Time was short, and I would have to get them out quickly to bars and restaurants. So in the cold blue dusk of December's waning days, I walked from bar to restaurant to bar, distributing the fliers and talking up the project with bartenders, restaurant managers, and waitstaff.

My spiel was quick. "Hi, I'm John Pollack," I'd say, handing them a flier. "I'm building the world's first cork boat. It's going to be a sixteen-foot Viking ship made entirely of wine and champagne corks, and I need your help to pull it off. Would you be willing to save your corks?"

The initial, reflexive response usually went something like this: the person would put down the stack of menus they were holding, or the glass they were wiping with a towel, and ask, "You're building a *what*?"

"A cork boat," I would explain, again. "The world's first cork boat."

"You mean a toy boat?"

"No, a real boat. A sixteen-foot Viking longboat. The plan is, when we're done, to sail it through French wine country." I didn't actually know if the boat would be sixteen feet, or if it would ever see France. But we were thinking big, and I spoke with total confidence. Still, a lot of people were perplexed. They couldn't figure out whether to take me seriously or not. I always gave them a few moments to ponder the possibility that, while I might be crazy, I *was* actually building the boat.

"You're serious?" came the response.

"I'm serious. And I really need your help—I can't drink enough on my own."

That usually got a laugh. When it didn't even get a chuckle, I knew I was in trouble.

The toney St. Regis Hotel on Sixteenth Street, a few blocks from the White House, was one place where my sense of humor fell short. The bar manager, a thin-lipped man in a double-breasted suit, practically sneered when I made my pitch. Handling the flier with his fingertips as if it were a soiled diaper, he refused to read it, instead setting it aside on the gleaming, black marble bar.

"I'll be sure to leave this for Nathan, so he can save more . . . *corks*," he said, sarcastically.

"Thanks. I appreciate that," I said. With great discipline, I resisted telling him to reach back and—if his arm were long enough—pull out the cork that was, apparently, stuck sideways deep up his ass.

It's not that I really cared about getting corks from the St. Regis, or any other particular establishment. The way I saw it, the opportunity to contribute corks to the world's first cork boat was just that—an opportunity, a chance to do something whimsically bold and have fun doing it. Those who didn't see that possibility were, well, missing the boat.

The St. Regis could decide to save or not save; I would understand if setting aside their corks was too much trouble. But I *was* angered by the man's blatant condescension. Even in a city that suffers from a chronic case of totem pole–itis (the reflexive habit of treating people according to their apparent rank on the totem pole of power), his attitude reeked.

Clearly, I wasn't an important person. Important people didn't build cork boats. Important people had power, or, at the very least, a good substitute: money. As I walked out, inwardly furious, I noticed that the leather-bound "books" lining the shelves of his bar were just like those at the Capitol— clever fakes.

Generally, though, people's responses to the boat were positive, even in places I wouldn't necessarily have expected. At the Toledo Lounge, a grungy dive in Adams Morgan that smells of cheap beer and cigarettes, the bar staff was fired up from the get-go. "We only go through five or six bottles of wine a week," said Christine, a bartender. "But we'll save the corks for you." Then, cocking her head flirtatiously, she asked: "Are you going to take me with you?"

Now, Christine was luscious and shapely, with big brown eyes and ringlets the color of ale cascading down her shoulders. I vowed then and there I'd definitely build a big boat, just to make room for her. "Absolutely," I said. "You can be an official cork maiden."

"You promise?"

I promised. Of course, five or six corks a week didn't amount to much, but that wasn't the point. Apart from the fact that she was a total flirt, I liked the fact that a bar inspired by a gritty Ohio city (and one only an hour south of Ann Arbor) was on board with the boat. Christine got it, in all its goofy greatness.

"Remember," I said as I walked out the door, "every cork counts!"

Adams Morgan is a diverse neighborhood in northwest Washington known for its raucous nightlife, and I worked it hard. The density of bars and restaurants on Eighteenth Street there is extraordinary—there must be sixty or seventy in a three-block stretch. Walking up one side of the street and down the other, I went into almost every establishment—Ethiopian, Italian, Indian, French, West African, Cajun, Vietnamese, Salvadoran, and Brazilian—that served wine.

If a lot of people didn't quite believe me, at least they humored my request for corks. With so many fliers out, New Year's Eve was bound to be a cork bonanza. When the big night finally came, I celebrated with a dozen friends on Capitol Hill. After cooking and consuming a banquet representing food from each of the past ten centuries, we trooped outside to bury a time capsule. The digging was a cold, dark, and muddy process, made all the messier by the late hour and too much champagne.

Our chosen capsule was a sturdy, cylindrical Tupperware container, sealed with silicone. In it, among other items from the twentieth century, were a cork from the evening's celebration and a flier for the boat. I wondered if, by the time the future finally arrived and somebody dug up our capsule, the cork boat would be history. Boat or no boat, I figured, at least people would know that at the turn of the century the spirit of creativity was alive and well.

A few days after New Year's, now gloriously free from nine-to-five responsibilities, I set off to collect corks, eager and expect-

ing a big haul. I even brought along several large sacks to
carry them all home.

I was in for a rude awakening. Despite a few enthusiastic
supporters, most people had blown it off. Some bartenders
were stubbornly indifferent. A lot of waitstaff had forgotten.
Others had dismissed me as a joker. Some just thought saving corks was a royal pain in the ass. And then there was the
competition. Apparently, a small but dedicated corps of arts-
and-crafters were collecting them for trivets, corkboards, and
wreaths, and had already put in their dibs.

"I already promised them . . . ," a bartender would say,
almost apologetically. I tried to cajole some into switching
sides. Help make a trivet, or help build the world's first cork
boat—was there even a choice? Think big, I'd say. Think Thor
Heyerdahl. Think epic journey. Don't think trivets. But few
were swayed.

Some sympathizers did look out for me; Christine, at the
Toledo Lounge, came through with her half-dozen. The Ira-
nian manager of I Matti, an Italian restaurant, had gathered
quite a few, too. And the maître d' at Ruth's Chris Steakhouse
in Dupont Circle called me at home a few days later. "I have
corks for you," she said, a little furtively. "I had to take them
from some guy saving for a corkboard. You'd better come by
this afternoon." Returning home with my haul, I counted out
her corks. She had snagged 327. At that moment, a single haul
of 327 seemed fantastic. But that number, I discovered, was
misleading. Some of the corks were plastic fakes. Others were

broken or moldy, and had to be thrown out. So in the grand scheme of things, my net haul was meager. Unfortunately, meager would soon become the norm.

In the months that followed, picking up corks became a task I put off as long as possible, often for weeks at a time. In fact, I came to loathe the chore. I had my routes, and I felt like an overgrown paperboy, except that I didn't get paid. The paper grocery sacks I carried held eleven hundred corks each, give or take a few. But it could take me two hours of prospecting to fill up a single bag.

Trudging from bar to bar through the February slush, I started asking myself: What the hell am I doing out here? What am I doing with my life?

Total freedom had looked so good from the confines of a job, but now that I had quit I wasn't so sure. All the surplus time I'd suddenly gained came at an unexpected cost—a lack of structure, a sense of isolation, and nagging doubts about my future. Sure, I had the cork boat project. But sometimes I felt like a total idiot, walking into hipster bars and fancy restaurants, asking for corks.

"How do you have time for this?" people would ask, often a little dismissively. "Don't you have a job?"

"I work for myself," I would answer, feigning confidence. "I'm a consultant."

Which was the truth, sort of. Mindful of my finances, I had lined up some consulting work—mainly writing Web copy for an Internet start-up. The dot-com's president had promised to pay top dollar. And he did, for about six weeks. Then, when the dot-com boom started to implode, the backers yanked their capital and the company filed for bankruptcy. A form letter suggested I consult with a lawyer regarding my final paycheck.

I did have some savings, and I lived modestly. My studio apartment in Dupont Circle was relatively cheap. But still, nothing was coming in, and the meter was running. Had I made a mistake, leaving behind a steady job with perks and benefits just to build a cork boat?

Whenever I got down, or whenever I scored a triumph, I would call my Aunt Marlene. She ran a bed-and-breakfast in Ludington, a small beach town on the shore of Lake Michigan. Given the nature of her business, I could usually count on finding her at home during the day, and she was never short on encouragement.

"Just keep going, Johnny," she'd say. "I know you can do it."

In her own way, Marlene was an organizer, too. For many years she had run a local dance studio and put on big, Broadway-style productions at the local community college. She was just as talented in the world of political fund-raising, cajoling, pulling, and teasing money out of people, appealing always to their better instincts. On one campaign, the other fund-raisers had nicknamed her "the green tornado." She had the magic touch, and her enthusiasm was contagious.

Even with her encouragement, though, I was losing steam.

The corks just weren't coming in fast enough. I was constantly updating the math, keeping a tally and calculating the incoming flow rate, so I could project a feasible construction schedule. My girlfriend at the time, Zoë, an analyst at the White House Office of Management and Budget, even helped me set up a spreadsheet to track them, by restaurant and month. But no matter how I ran the numbers, or how aggressively I collected, that schedule kept receding into the future.

I was starting to get frustrated with Garth, too. While he was still enthusiastic about the project, he never seemed to have time to collect corks. "Look, I have a job," he reminded me more than once. What could I say?

But then, inevitably, somewhere along one of my routes, I'd get a little spark of encouragement that kept me going. In Cities, an upscale bar catering to Washington's wealthy Eurotrash, I overheard one of the hostesses—dressed in a little black dress no matter what the weather—whisper to a friend, "There he is! That's the cork guy. He's building a boat out of wine corks."

Or I'd pull up a stool at Nora's, a gourmet organic restaurant, where Jack, the wine steward and barkeep, would pour me a glass of beer, on the house. "How's the boat?" Jack would always ask, a little gruffly. "It's coming along," I'd answer, mustering an optimistic tone even if I was down. I always had an update ready—the latest cork tally, some factoid about corks, or a napkin sketch of the latest design. Jack, a bear of a man who built wooden kayaks in his spare time, always had a big bucket of corks waiting for me. Good quality corks, too—none of those agglomerates, made up of compressed bits and pieces glued together, or worse yet, the plastic ones. Although there were some exceptions, most fine wines—especially fine organic wines—didn't come with plastic corks.

As I had discovered early in my rounds, the plastic cork was making steady inroads against its natural rival, and had sparked a nasty debate that the press was calling the "Cork Wars." PLASTIC STOPPERS UNCORK GREAT WINE DEBATE, read one headline. SOUR GRAPES read another. With consumers buying fourteen billion bottles of wine a year, there was a lot at stake. An organization called the World Cork Congress had even scheduled a summit, later in the year, to discuss and counter the attacks of the plastic-cork partisans.

According to these synthetic-cork boosters, their product was superior because it eliminated spoilage from the cork-related microbial growth known as 2-4-6 Trichloranisole, or "cork taint." According to their data, cork taint was ruining up to ten percent of all bottled wine and cost vintners tens of millions of dollars every year. A British supermarket chain, reacting to criticism after it leaned on its suppliers to switch to plastic corks, sent customers a letter complaining of "greedy" cork farmers, whom they accused of environmental degradation.

Angered, cork traditionalists fired back with their own laboratory data on cork taint, and other rebuttals. "First the supermarkets said that cork was overpriced. Then they said it spoilt wine. Now they say cork-stripping is an environmental hazard," Paulo Portas, a prominent Portuguese politician, told the *Guardian*. "This is a campaign based on falsehoods."

As all the articles explained, producing corks doesn't require cutting down even a single tree. Rather, corks are punched from sheets of bark carefully stripped, once every nine years, from the *Quercus suber,* a species of oak that grows throughout Mediterranean countries, but principally in Portugal. Carefully tended by foresters from generation to generation, each tree usually produces about four thousand corks per harvest, and can live for more than two hundred years.

With whole villages depending on these cork forests for their livelihood, environmentalists, in fact, commended them for protecting some of the last remaining habitat for several of Europe's endangered species—including the wild boar, the Iberian lynx, and Spain's imperial eagle.

The exchanges were getting nasty. One birdwatcher wrote a letter to the editor urging Malcolm Gluck, a British wine writer, to shut his mouth with a plastic stopper. In his next column, Gluck lashed back at the "misinformed bird lover," directing him to a Somerfield Argentine Sangiovese with the wry observation that "it'd be marvelous with a roast bird."

Whatever the relative merits of plastic corks might be, my own anecdotal evidence—based largely on conversations with bartenders—suggested that the drinking public, given a choice, would almost always choose natural corks over their

plastic rivals. I knew I would: part of wine's appeal is its aura
of tradition, and the subtle sense of ceremony that accompa-
nies the soft, musical *thwock* of a pulled cork. Extracting a
plastic stopper just sort of drains all the romance from a bottle before a single drop of wine even splashes into the glass.

Still, plastic corks were making inroads. And when I mentioned to Garth that press reports had identified billionaire
software mogul Bill Gates as a principal investor in the world's
leading plastic-cork company, that put him over the edge.

"Death to the plastic cork!" he shouted, gleefully. I agreed a
hundred percent, and joked that our boat could serve as the
flagship of an entire cork navy, one that would defend against
the evil, bobbing armada of synthetic invaders. That is, if we
could ever collect enough corks to build the damned thing.

We certainly didn't lack for input and advice. All along my
cork routes, the bartenders, waitstaff, and restaurateurs who
saved for me were often eager to share their ideas about construction. "You should drill holes through them and wire
them together," one said. "I think you should grind them up
and mix them with epoxy," said another. "How about gluing
them to boards, or using nails?" No matter how impractical
their ideas sometimes seemed, I always listened politely. After
all, I myself didn't exactly appear to be a champion of common sense, either.

Most people just couldn't get over the fact that we were
designing it from scratch. "But what plans are you going to

use?" they kept asking, even when I explained that there were no plans because the cork boat simply had no precedent.

I had certainly searched for one, though. I spent hours on the Web, chasing down false leads on children's bath toys and rowing clubs from Ireland's County Cork until my eyes were bleary. But I also looked the old-fashioned way: I applied for a library card and burrowed into the biggest and most comprehensive collection of books, maps, and manuscripts ever assembled in human history, the Library of Congress.

I did my research in the Adams Building, an art deco monument of white marble and heavy bronze doors, just down the street from the back door of the Supreme Court, on Capitol Hill. I parked myself at a long oak table in one of its cavernous reading rooms, pausing to appreciate the soaring ceilings and panoramic murals commemorating the library's principal founder, Thomas Jefferson. High above me, one of his quotes caught my eye: "The ground of Liberty is to be gained by inches. We must be contented to secure what we can get from time to time and eternally press forward for what is yet to get."

I knew Jefferson wasn't referring to cork boats when he wrote that. But still, he was both inventor and oenophile, and I gave myself license to interpret his words as my needs required. Like liberty, the cork boat was to be gained by inches—1.5 inches at a time, to be precise. And I had to keep pressing forward if I ever hoped to see my vessel afloat.

Eager to find what I could, I asked a librarian where I might find the reference books on boatbuilding, and was directed to the proper shelf, not far from a pair of carved stone owls that kept a sharp watch over the dictionary stands. Soon I was happily engrossed in encyclopedic definitions and drawings of every imaginable type of watercraft, from the lighter-than-balsa ambatch raft of the Nile valley to the dugout *zoppolo* of the Dalmatian coast, and everything in between. I was so enchanted by the ingenuity and resourcefulness of my fellow boatbuilders through the ages that it took a lot of discipline to set aside the fun historical stuff to inspect— reluctantly—a more turgid academic volume entitled *Naval Architecture for Non-Naval Architects.*

The author's preface was rather stern. "If floating craft play any sort of role in your work or hobby, you are well advised to teach yourself something of their capabilities and limitations . . . ," he wrote. Did that mean I absolutely had to understand such vital topics as "hydrostatic curves," "model basin theory," and the "mensuration of hull forms"? No, I decided, I would rather be shipwrecked. Feeling a little guilty, though, I photocopied what looked like a few critical pages, and promised myself I would read them later. In all fairness, though, the book did yield one tangentially relevant tidbit: the origin of the word *ton.*

Apparently, way back in the 1400s, the king of England grew frustrated with shippers who were avoiding the crown's duty on wine by misstating volumes and other chicanery.

Determined to collect his tax, he ordered that all wine arriving from the Continent be shipped in standardized, 252-gallon casks called "tuns," to be counted one by one as sailors unloaded them at the wharf. Consequently, a ship's size—or tonnage—was judged by the number of tuns, or barrels, it could hold. Filled with wine, each of these barrels weighed 2,240 pounds, a weight known today in England as the long ton, which is slightly heavier than the short ton, its more familiar 2,000-pound American cousin.

Not that any of these facts really helped me. Regretfully, I had to concede that my naval research, while interesting, was running aground. Pursuing a new direction, I turned my attention from boat design to building materials, specifically cork. And I soon discovered that cork had a fascinating history in its own right. Apparently, the pharaohs of ancient Egypt were the first people to use the bark to seal jugs and bottles, and they recorded their innovation in stone hieroglyphs. Centuries later, Greek traders used cork to close clay amphorae as they plied the stormy seas of the known world.

But then, with the fall of Rome, a veil of ignorance fell over Europe, and the humble cork was forgotten. Although people still drank wine in great quantities, they sealed their jugs with oily rags, wooden plugs, and other small objects.

It was a blind Benedictine monk, Dom Pérignon, who rediscovered the cork stopper sometime in the 1660s. A vintner of great devotion, he had turned to cork after becoming frustrated by traditional wooden stoppers that, wrapped in oiled hemp, kept popping out of his bottles prematurely under pressure from the bubbly.

Coincidentally, the English scientist Robert Hooker was marveling at cork around the same time. Peering through a novel invention called the microscope, Hooker discovered that cork was composed of millions of tiny air pockets separated by thin walls. This microscopic matrix reminded him of cells in a monastery, and a new biological concept—the *cell*—was born.

As much as I loved discovering such historical trivia, though, I still hadn't answered the central question: How to build the boat? The closest I came was a somewhat cryptic reference to traditional rafts made of cork bark in northern Portugal, used to collect seaweed and stalk octopi across shallow, rocky tidal flats. But as far as I could determine, nobody in the past ten thousand years of human watercraft had ever built a boat from individual corks. So while we could surely borrow ideas from previous craft, the cork boat itself would ultimately be a novel creation. And I liked that. We would just have to start experimenting.

UNGLUED

G arth had convinced me, in a small-scale test, that we couldn't just stuff loose corks into net bags, or even into a net tube we sewed ourselves. At least not if we wanted our boat to have any structure: if the corks were loose, the whole thing would flop like a garden hose. "We need more structural strength," he insisted. "If the corks aren't in some orderly array, it won't work."

We also needed an orderly way to store our corks. Although we were still far short of our goal, I had collected more than 32,000, and they kept spilling from the growing number of paper grocery sacks in both my apartment and Garth's bedroom, in his nearby group house. Paper bags, though somewhat unstable, had one main advantage: they allowed the corks to breathe. One week in a plastic bag or closed container made the damp used corks go moldy. And if there was one thing I found more irksome than collecting the corks, it was having to throw them out. If that meant accidentally knocking over the occasional paper bag, sending a cascade of corks across the floor, I'd just have to live with that.

Still, the numbers were mounting and we needed a workshop. In an expensive city like Washington, this wasn't easy. We pursued every possibility, from a local wine store, to a liquor distributor's warehouse, to the garages of good friends who, for some reason, all seemed reluctant to surrender their parking spots. Desperate, we even tried to rent the fallout shelter deep beneath the Envoy, the 1950s-era apartment building where Brandt lived. But his landlord ignored our pitch letter and failed to return Brandt's repeated phone calls.

Despite this acute lack of space, I kept working my cork routes, hauling home bag after bag. But since Garth's bedroom was bigger than my entire apartment, he bore the brunt of storage. Soon, sacks containing tens of thousands of corks teetered toward his ceiling, threatening to spill at the slightest provocation.

Meanwhile, we kept experimenting with different ways to attach the corks. Early on, we discovered a form that seemed quite promising: a single upright cork, surrounded by six others in a concentric ring, formed a hexagon. It was a shape that seemed both stable and scalable; that is, we could add concentric rings of cork around the initial hexagon to create hexagonal units of larger and larger diameter.

Theoretically, we could stack these on top of each other to form a hexagonal log. Sewn into a strong fishnet tube, the hexagonal log should, we reasoned, hold its form. But how were we going to hold the individual corks together? The consequences of failure were potentially dire. After talking through the pros and cons of superglue, wood glue, and epoxy, Garth suggested we try using a hot glue gun. I had no idea what a hot glue gun was, but it sounded fun. That is, until a few nights later, when I tried one.

Vaguely pistol-shaped and tethered by its cord to an electrical outlet, a glue gun melts dry sticks of glue into a messy liquid roughly the consistency of honey, only hotter. So much hotter, in fact, that a stray dribble on your skin can produce not only an excruciating second-degree burn, but also the longest, sharpest string of expletives ever uttered in a single breath.

Cursing and laughing into the night, we glued and glued and glued. At one point we even came up with a refinement to the process—extruding the middle cork in each cluster, so that it resembled the cork equivalent of a single-nubbed Lego. This made the vertical attachment of each cluster a simple matter of stacking, much like vertebrae in a backbone.

At first, we were quite taken with our little innovation. It was exciting to create order from chaos and finally see so many corks become one. But at the same time, I worried that it was taking too long. Gluing each "vertebra" was proving to be a slow process. A *very* slow process.

Sometime after midnight, I timed Garth gluing at top speed, then punched up some figures on a calculator. The results were disheartening: it would take the two of us more than a year's worth of eight-hour days to glue 100,000 corks together. And that wasn't even counting the preliminary process of sorting corks, which was absolutely vital. Because the truth was, of all those I collected, maybe only half were good enough to use in the boat. A significant number of the corks coming in were plastic, and we weren't building a plastic boat. Almost as bad were the agglomerates, which, according to my countertop tests, soaked up water like a sponge.

A few days later, Garth made a declaration. "Used corks are a waste of time," he said. I bristled, a little sensitive, perhaps, about just whose time was being wasted. But I heard him out. As hard as it was to admit, I knew he might be right.

"Look. We're going to need a lot of corks," he continued. "Let's just get them from Cork Supply USA."

Cork Supply USA, located in Benicia, California, is one of America's leading cork importers. I had found the company on the Web a few months earlier. I had even sent them an e-mail inquiring about potential support for the project, and they hadn't dismissed the possibility. Apparently, the owner, a cork entrepreneur named Jochen Michalski, thought the boat sounded interesting.

But despite Garth's reasoning, I was still reluctant to use virgin corks. I liked the concept of building the boat with used corks from thousands of different people, many stained burgundy and rich with personal memories. Every used cork had a story to tell; bringing those stories together was an inherent source of the boat's appeal. Another source lay in engaging a lot of people, through their donations. Accepting corks from a cork company smacked of cheating.

On the other hand, maybe I was being too much of a purist. I was sick of working those cork routes, especially on my own. And it didn't look like I would be able to collect enough used corks, period. At least not in time to build a boat anytime in the near future. And who said there were any rules about building a cork boat, anyway? Wasn't this supposed to be fun?

So the next day I got on the phone with Cork Supply's business manager, a fellow named Chris Sipola, and asked him if his company would be willing to support the project with a sizable donation of corks. "I might need a lot of corks," I warned him. "Eventually, say, as many as . . . sixty thousand. Does that number faze you?" I paused, bracing myself for the worst.

"Look," Sipola said, "I'm sitting in a warehouse with sixty million corks. No, that number doesn't faze me."

And so, a few weeks later, a brown UPS van pulled up in front of my brownstone to deliver three big cardboard boxes, each the size of a washing machine. Since these were virgin corks that had never been squeezed into the neck of a bottle, they took up a lot more volume than those I had been collecting locally; each box was labeled 5,000 CORKS. Excited, I lugged them, one by one, up the four flights to my apartment.

I cut open the first box with a knife, feeling a little like Edmond Dantes in *The Count of Monte Cristo* opening those treasure chests for the first time. It was as if I had just been released from prison, had won the cork lottery, or both at once. I was suddenly the proud owner of fifteen thousand virgin corks—perfect, cylindrical corks. Buoyant about my new-found wealth, my antipathy toward virgin corks vanished in an instant. Like a fine sherry blended from different vintages, I reasoned, the world's first cork boat would be a blend of old and new.

Energized, I got on the phone to recruit a team of volunteers. I wanted to see how many corks a half-dozen people could glue together in a single day. Maybe if we set up an assembly line like Henry Ford, we could blitz out glued corks by the thousand.

Saturday arrived gray and gloomy, and I worried about turnout. But one by one, my six cork recruits showed up at Garth's house, where he had prepared a workspace by taping down several layers of newspaper over his landlord's dining room table. After explaining the intricacies of glue guns to the assembled team of international policy experts, editors, federal budget analysts, and legislative staff, we got right to work. None, of course, were boatbuilders. But all were fast learners.

With two volunteers setting up corks and six of us working our glue guns, we pushed hard through a long day. Due to the presence of a volunteer's three-year-old daughter, we did our best to stifle our burn-induced curses. For speed's sake, we glued the corks end to end to end, forming long rods that

Garth and I intended to bundle into hexagons later. As I thought they might, people enjoyed the mindless work and chatted away.

"It's like raking leaves," said my friend Michele Rivard, declaring her satisfaction. "You can see exactly what you've gotten done."

That was certainly true. But I could also see what we *hadn't* gotten done. Despite our efforts, we hadn't gotten through a single box.

Unplugging the glue guns, Garth and I thanked everyone profusely for their help and declared the day a success. Intuitively, however, I knew that the underlying math was ugly. Even with a bigger team, gluing 100,000 corks together would require at least four thousand hours. And there was little chance that my friends, who were politely nursing their burns as they walked out, would be eager or willing to return for weekend after weekend of punishment. So we were back, quite literally, to the drawing board.

In the week or so that followed, Garth and I sketched out several other approaches. If our goal was to find a way to load corks into mesh tubes in an orderly array, why couldn't we just skip the glue and devise a tubular loading system? A tight cluster of very narrow pipes that slipped directly into a mesh tube might enable us to feed corks into position relatively quickly. All we'd have to do, theoretically, would be to slide corks into the piping until the system was full, tip the array vertically, and slowly withdraw the pipes. If we did it carefully, we could cinch the netting tightly around the corks as they emerged.

As with the glue-gun fiasco, this was easier said than done. Even as I tinkered with a homemade prototype, I priced out different kinds of piping and customized cardboard tubes. But when the prototype failed, neither seemed worth the required investment. And so we dropped the idea of the tubular loading system, too. Gradually, I was starting to appreciate why nobody had ever built a cork boat before. Maybe it was impossible.

"You don't have to build this boat," Zoë reassured me, after listening to my woes for the umpteenth time. "Or you could build a smaller boat. Just remember, you're not a failure if you decide you'd rather spend your time doing something else."

But what else was I going to do? Admit defeat, put on a suit and tie, and go looking for a job again? No, I couldn't bear that. I may have been a little despondent, but I wasn't desperate. At least not yet.

STRETCHING THE LIMITS

A few weeks later, anxious and frustrated, I sat down at my kitchen table and spread out several dozen corks. As much as anything else, these solo work sessions were an effort at conscious distraction. Manipulating corks always seemed to engage another part of my brain, one that gave me temporary relief from a crescendo of doubt growing stronger by the day.

Thoughts whirling, I reached for a handful of corks and started arranging them into the standard hexagonal vertebra. What should I do with myself? Was the whole boat project just a dead end? Should I get a job? Stop thinking, I told myself. Just stop thinking. Focus on the corks. Completing the first hexagon, I reached for another handful, but jostled the table, knocking over the first vertebra and sending a cascade of corks pattering onto the floor.

"Damn these corks!" I muttered, crawling under the rickety table to retrieve the last of my escapees. Irritated, I fetched a few rubber bands from my desk. I wasn't about to spend my whole afternoon chasing corks across the floor. Stretching one open with my fingertips, I stuck seven corks inside, then slipped my fingers out. Immediately it contracted to form a perfectly snug hexagonal cluster. Interesting.

I tried it again. Once more, at the very instant I withdrew my fingertips, the stretched band contracted around the corks to bring them into tight hexagonal formation. This really was interesting. Would other configurations work? I gave them a try. Three corks in a rubber band formed a triangle, but it wasn't scalable; as I slipped more corks inside the band, the arrangement became asymmetrical and unstable, shifting under compression.

One by one, I kept adding corks to see if I could restore balance to the grouping. When I stuck the seventh cork in, the cluster stabilized again, into the original hexagon (a six-cork ring encircling a seventh cork). Getting excited, I grabbed more corks and kept going. At eight, nine, ten, eleven, twelve corks, and beyond, the grouping lacked symmetry and stability. It didn't regain stability until I added the nineteenth cork, when the rubber band brought the cluster into hexagonal form once again. While I didn't understand the underlying mathematics of what I was seeing, I intuitively grasped that rubber bands could potentially save us enormous assembly time. Was this the breakthrough we had been looking for?

I called Garth at work to get his opinion.

"Rubber bands!" he said, after I explained the phenomenon. "That's brilliant!"

To be honest, I wasn't so sure. Even within the context of building a cork boat, the notion of using ordinary rubber bands to attach a hundred thousand corks seemed like, well, a stretch. But Garth insisted that the rubber-band idea was worth pursuing; he said it was an efficient, practical, affordable solution that was—just as important—technically elegant. Good architecture is all about how things are put together, he said. And since we were planning to sheathe our cork logs in fishnet, the rubber bands wouldn't have to bear any appreciable strain over the long term. They were just for temporary, though critical, cork alignment.

It was worth a try. So the next day I walked down to my neighborhood Office Depot to buy rubber bands. I had never really paid much attention to rubber bands before, and there were a lot of options—big, small, wide, narrow, and in a rainbow of colors, too. I bought a bag of assorted bands for $3.59, plus tax, and headed home. Its label boasted "a band for every purpose." We would certainly put that claim to the test.

Over the next couple of days, Garth and I tried every kind of band in the bag. Not only was this new assembly process lightning fast compared to our previous efforts, it didn't cause second-degree burns, either. Even the color of the corks and the rubber bands matched. From a short distance, the khaki bands virtually disappeared against the tan cork. Somehow, in my frustration, it seemed I might have stumbled onto the perfect solution.

Making some quick calculations, Garth and I estimated

that we would need about fifteen thousand rubber bands. Although rubber bands were relatively cheap, so were we. We had found a cork company to donate corks; why not get a rubber-band company to sponsor the boat, too? Searching the fine print on our original package of bands, I quickly found the Web address for the Alliance Rubber Company, in Hot Springs, Arkansas. Logging on for more information, I soon found myself tangled in rubber-band trivia.

Rubber trees, I learned, grow up to fifty feet tall, produce an average of nineteen pounds of rubber sap a year, and can be tapped for up to twenty-eight years. And although Christopher Columbus caused a minor sensation when he brought rubber balls back to Spain from the West Indies in 1496, more than three centuries passed before a London coach-maker transformed the material into the world's first rubber bands, in 1823.

Following its invention, the humble rubber band languished, underutilized, for a century. Then, one windy day in 1923, an Ohio entrepreneur named William H. Spencer saw a newspaper blowing down the street and had an epiphany: Why not recycle scrap rubber from Akron's tire plants into rubber bands and have paperboys use them to secure the papers on their daily rounds?

This was a novel use for rubber bands, and one with a potentially huge market. Spencer's first customer was the publisher of the *Akron Beacon Journal,* and every one of the paper's home delivery customers was soon, albeit unwittingly, purchasing a rubber band with every paper that landed on their porch. Oklahoma's *Tulsa World* followed suit, and the idea started catching on across the country. This being the heyday of newspapers, it was an elastic market.

But Spencer wasn't satisfied. Having conquered the world of newspapers, he also convinced area grocers to trade in their rough twine for rubber bands, a packaging innovation that helped speed and simplify the bundling of carrots, celery, and other vegetables. This idea, too, spread quickly. Soon enough, Spencer's enterprise, the Alliance Rubber Company, was selling millions and millions of rubber bands.

I saw my opening and reached for the phone. Calling cold, I explained to the receptionist who I was and what I was building. She transferred me to a manager, who listened patiently as I repeated the reason for my call. My pitch was simple but bold. "The Alliance Rubber Company was founded on innovation," I said. "The world's first cork boat—bound with rubber bands—exemplifies that same tradition."

Sensing a glimmer of possibility in the fact that she didn't hang up on me, I pressed my case. "You know, a lot of people take rubber bands for granted these days. This boat would be a great showcase to highlight your product's incredible versatility, especially as I expect we'll get a lot of press attention at the launch. Your company would be the perfect sponsor. Would you be willing to donate the bands we need?"

As it turned out, the company, in addition to its tradition of innovation, had a penchant for charity. It had once supported a Delaware mailroom clerk's attempt to build the world's biggest rubber-band ball, a behemoth that topped out at over 2,500 pounds.

Still, the company had never heard of anybody using rubber bands to assemble a boat, let alone one built of wine corks. It was a crazy idea, she said, but it sounded like fun. She would speak with the president. A few weeks later, after an exchange of e-mails and some cursory tests of sample bands, a UPS driver rang my bell with a delivery from Arkansas— several hefty cartons of tangled rubber spaghetti. Gleeful, I scrawled my signature on his electronic pad and carried the boxes, one by one, upstairs to my apartment.

We had requested the bands in two sizes: five thousand of the short, wide number 64, and ten thousand of its long and skinny cousin, the glorious 117-B. The long bands— longer than any I had ever seen—would be our perimeter bands, capable of compressing and securing hexagonal 127-cork disks that were roughly the diameter of a dinner plate. We would use the short bands to bind the disks vertically, one atop the other, into logs. We weren't sure exactly how to do that yet, but it didn't matter. We would figure it out.

Over the course of the next week, I managed to assemble an experimental eight-foot hexagonal log on the floor of my apartment, improvising with dozens of the number 64 bands to attach the disks longitudinally. I was pleased with my handiwork, but when Garth stopped by after work one day to check it out, the instantaneous look on his face said it all—lame.

In all honesty, I knew the log had problems. Although the individual disks were solid, the assembly as a whole was unstable—its longitudinal banding knotted, uneven, and ugly. But as Garth went through only the most cursory motions of examining it, then stood to leave again with hardly a word, my blood pressure surged. If he had a better method in mind, I was all ears. But I didn't hear any forthcoming solutions, or even any encouragement. Instead, all I felt was the silent sting of condescension.

I didn't want an architectural critic. I wanted a partner, one who was willing to put in the time to make the boat a physical reality, not one content with a hypothetical, would-be craft to be constructed sometime in the distant future. And while we had never discussed the terms of our partnership explicitly, I had always assumed, fairly or unfairly, that we would invest roughly the same amount of sweat equity in the project. But maybe, as I was discovering belatedly, those assumptions were just that. Whatever the case, I was so furious and frustrated that when Garth walked out, I felt like kicking the log to pieces. But I had put in too many hours, and held myself in check.

Seeking solace, I called Zoë. A gifted listener, she was sympathetic. To cheer me up, she volunteered to help me figure out a better banding system. "There's got to be a way," she insisted. As an undergraduate at Yale, Zoë had majored in architecture. She had gone on to get a master's in public policy from Harvard, then back to Yale for a law degree. In short, she was a brainiac whose abstract problem-solving skills were off the charts. If she thought we could figure out a uniform, interlocking banding pattern, we probably could. It was the kind of brain-teaser she excelled at solving.

Her confidence was all I needed. The next weekend, after six or seven hours working through various combinations and patterns, we hit upon an elegant system of leapfrogging, overlapping bands that, at least in theory, would allow us to build uniform logs of unlimited length and significant strength. I dubbed it the Zoë Banding System.

Even Garth loved it. "Nice work!" he said. And he meant it. The Zoë Banding System was a clean and consistent interlocking hook-and-ladder pattern that enabled us to build flexible, spinelike columns of cork disks. It was a big breakthrough, and we both knew it.

Finally the project was gaining momentum. Yes, it was mid-June, and the summertime launch we had touted on our SAVE YOUR CORKS flier was no longer feasible. But an autumn launch was still possible. We had more than 48,000 corks on hand, and a sponsor willing to supply more. We had enough rubber bands to bungee-jump off the Empire State Building. We had located suitable netting from a supplier in Florida; and we had developed a working knowledge of the boat's basic components.

"If we can find a workshop," I said, "we might be able to get the boat into the water on Columbus Day."

Garth insisted that my schedule was overly ambitious. "We've still got too much to figure out," he said. "We should work on it over the winter and launch next summer."

I pushed back. Deep down, I worried that if we put off the launch for a year we might lose all our momentum. "Come on, Garth," I said. "If we both really bust ass for the next three or four months, we can get it done. It's totally possible."

"No, we don't have enough time," he said. Even if it were possible, he added, he wasn't prepared to spend his entire summer working on the boat. He had some climbing trips he wanted to take.

We argued. We got nowhere. It wasn't as if Garth didn't feel a strong stake in the project. Obviously he did, or he'd just pull out altogether and tell me, "It's your boat, do whatever you want." Still, if Garth wasn't willing to let go, neither was he willing to dive in, like I wanted.

Anger, doubt, and guilt fought a pitched battle within me. I knew I was asking a lot of him, but no more than I was demanding of myself. Still, was I being unreasonable, even selfish, in setting our construction schedule? Maybe so. The boat was my dream, after all, not his. But emotion trumped reason, and I had grown jealous watching him pull frequent all-nighters at his job. Over the past ten months, in fact, I had come to understand exactly how he worked: only looming deadlines made him focus. But whether he would ever throw himself into our project with the zeal I sought, I couldn't be sure. As a mutual friend put it, Garth was by his very nature "immune to calendar, clock, and reality." One thing had become clear: if I didn't keep driving the project forward, the cork boat would languish unfinished, forever.

SHIP OF STATE

A s things turned out, my own priorities were about to shift radically. I was caught completely off guard answering my phone a few weeks later.

"Hello, John? This is Josh Gottheimer from the White House."

It took a brief moment for the words "White House" to sink in. I hadn't spoken with Josh in over a year, but I could guess why he was calling. "Hey, how's it going?" I said casually, my heart pounding.

"Fine. Listen, Lowell Weiss is leaving. We need somebody to fill his slot. Would you be interested?"

My mind raced. I had met Lowell. Like Josh, he was a speechwriter for President Clinton. One of six. I had tried for several years to get a job in that office, even as I worked on the Hill. Getting to the White House, in fact, had been one of my biggest professional goals in coming to Washington. I'd come close twice, but got beaten out both times. Now, like a frost-bitten climber defeated on several attempts to summit a tough mountain, I wasn't sure I had the stomach for yet another dubious assault. I didn't think I could endure one more do-or-die writing test, or another round of interrogation, only to be rejected a third time. Besides, it would totally sink the cork boat for the year.

"Yes, of course I would," I said.

"Great. Could you come in this afternoon?"

I countered with tomorrow, and twenty-four hours later found myself back in the dread suit and tie, sitting on the edge of a chair in a cramped West Wing office. I watched Terry Edmonds, the President's chief speechwriter, as he studied my newly updated résumé.

I'd never met Edmonds before, but I had done what last-minute research I could on the Web. At forty-nine, he was an American success story, proof that the American Dream was alive and well. He had grown up in public housing in Baltimore, the son of a truck driver and a waitress, to become the first African-American Presidential speechwriter in American history. Even among the best, apparently, he was considered a gifted writer.

Waiting for him to speak, I tried to think reassuring thoughts: If I get the job, great. If I don't, fine. Just don't screw this up.

After what seemed like forever, Edmonds pushed his glasses up to the top of his head. "I am very impressed by your background," he said. "I have no doubt you can do the job." My heart almost skipped a beat.

"But you have a lot of other"—he paused, as if searching for the right word—"projects." He wanted to know about my cork boat.

I had added the boat to my résumé the night before, on an impulse. It was the last line, under the category of Other, and read: "Currently building the world's first cork boat."

I quickly explained the evolution of the project, but omitted mention of my frequent doubts, frustrations, and the fact that it was consuming more hours than I dared tally. Instead, I spoke about the creative impulse it revealed, and assured him that, if offered a job at the White House, I would certainly suspend construction for the duration of my tenure. Speechwriting for the President would be my first and only priority.

He seemed satisfied with my answer, at least for the moment. We went on to discuss politics and poetry, and how they intersect in speechwriting. As the conversation went on, I began to think I might have a shot. But something was on my mind, and as the interview wound down, I had to ask—was there a writing test he wanted me to take?

No, Edmonds said. He had seen my writing, and liked it. But he wanted me to meet with the rest of the speechwriters, so they could weigh in. He'd have Josh call to set up a time.

Two days later, I was back for the meeting, and found myself, once again, explaining the cork boat. Again, I addressed concerns about my time commitments. Not a problem, I reassured them. I would put the boat on hold. They also wanted to know about my victory at the 1995 World Pun Championships, in Austin, Texas, which I had also listed on my résumé. Laughing, I gave them a quick recap of the annual tournament.

The annual contest is set up in a single-elimination format, the competitors pairing off in front of a judge, a time-keeper, and a large, hooting audience. Given a topic, the first competitor has five seconds to make a pun on that topic; the second competitor has five seconds to respond; and then the two hurl puns back and forth until someone fails to make a pun before the five-second deadline. The best pun I made all day was on the topic of flying machines. When my opponent, a former champion, accused me of "winging it," I just turned my head and calmly replied, "U-2?" The crowd went wild. Advancing through five brutal rounds to defeat a paramedic on the topic of "external body parts," I flew home to Michigan with the champion's trophy: a gilded horse's ass.

Looking around the room at my incredulous interviewers, I suddenly worried that I had lost them, that I had come across as too weird to work at the White House. Racing to recover, I made a quick connection: "Punning is all about hearing how words sound," I said. "Isn't that central to good speechwriting?"

They said they'd get back to me.

One day dragged into two. Two days became a week. Had I said something terribly wrong?

To kill time one afternoon and work off my anxiety, I built

an enormous cork hexagon, the largest we had yet attempted: 169 corks. I also kept collecting, and listened impatiently as a carpet salesman on one of my cork routes insisted—absolutely insisted—that I needed an aluminum frame for the boat. "You should just glue the corks to an aluminum boat," he said. "You need structure." All I could do was nod gravely, trying to imply I would consider his advice.

The next day, Zoë broke up with me. Ours had been an on-again, off-again relationship since we had started dating six months earlier, but the breakup wasn't exactly reassuring, under the circumstances. Maybe my luck was running out.

That Sunday, while I was at the gym, Edmonds left a message on my answering machine—no substance, just that I should call him back. I did, but he was unavailable. The suspense was killing me. I was discovering that I really, really wanted that job.

The phone rang first thing Monday morning. It was Edmonds. I steeled myself for the worst—a third and final rejection. "Well, we spoke with the President about you, and with John, and, at least on paper, you're the best candidate." John was John Podesta, the President's chief of staff. I had the job.

Trying to contain my jubilation, I thanked him as professionally as I could and made arrangements to start within the week. Hanging up, I let out a whoop. My first instinct was to call my parents, but they were on a ship somewhere off the coast of Greenland. So I called my Aunt Marlene, my confidante and biggest fan. She screamed with excitement. I had hit the big time.

The next day I found myself sitting in the basement of the West Wing, at a staff meeting of my fellow speechwriters. Suppressing the impulse to grin, I kept telling myself, Pay attention. Pay attention.

Apparently, there had been another finalist competing for the job, a speechwriter for the secretary of defense who had more experience than I. Already working within the administration, he was the safe choice. I was more of a wild card, and Edmonds confessed that he had debated whether or not to take a chance on me. Who is this guy with the cork boat? he wondered. Is he for real?

Ultimately, the cork boat—and the pun championship—had tipped the decision in my favor. After all the hard times at the White House, the speechwriting staff decided it needed a colleague with some levity. Even the President, who made the final decision, had liked the pun championship. On the decision memo recommending my hire, it was the only thing he circled, scribbling "Good!" in the margin.

"We're all counting on you to keep it light," Edmonds told me, at the end of the meeting. Mara Silver, his assistant, handed me a thick stack of paperwork to fill out. The FBI would be running an extensive background check for my security clearance, but I would be starting work immediately. And there was a lot of work to be done; the President was scheduled to present the nation's highest civilian award, the Medal of Freedom, to fifteen men and women in a few days, and I was to write several of their citations. It was a slow pitch, as first assignments go—I even knew one of the honorees, a family friend, Millie Jeffrey—but I still had to hit it out of the park.

Collecting my papers, I walked out of the West Wing and up the granite steps of the Old Executive Office Building, known as the OEOB, where I had been given a small office. It was an extremely narrow room with a beat-up desk and coffee-stained chair, a frayed couch, a computer, and a TV. Its only window, a grimy one at that, looked into an air shaft. I loved it.

"If you tip it on its side, it's a pretty big office," said Heather Hurlburt, the speechwriter whose office was right next door. I looked up. The ceiling was somewhere in the neighborhood of sixteen feet. Lofty ceilings for lofty words, I thought.

One other architectural detail caught my eye—the finely detailed doorknob that graced its heavy, mahogany door. It was cast in brass, with an anchor motif symbolizing the United States Navy. I guessed that it was a legacy of the OEOB's nineteenth-century origins as the State, War, and Navy Building. Given my nautical proclivities, I took the anchor as a good sign, and sat down to work.

Rummaging through the detritus of my desk drawer in search of some paper, I came across a notepad embossed in gold with the Presidential seal and the words ABOARD AIR

FORCE ONE. Wow, I thought, for the umpteenth time. This job is the real deal. I'd better not screw it up.

Shoving aside my doubts, I dug into my assignment. I spent the next several days distilling reams of material into brief paragraphs of concise eloquence, which the President delivered with his customary easy confidence at the ceremony. During the reception afterward, in the State Dining Room of the White House, I approached one of the honorees—World War II veteran, former senator, and onetime Presidential candidate George McGovern.

Congratulating him on his Medal of Freedom, I introduced myself as one of the President's speechwriters and told him about the wagon-borne bake sale I had helped organize on his behalf in 1972. "It was my first campaign, and I want to thank you for giving me my start in politics," I said. McGovern was gracious, if a bit distracted. But I didn't care; I was just thrilled to be working at the White House.

I had been given few instructions about my job, apart from the rudiments of the editing and approval process, and the fact that the President liked his speeches double-spaced, in 23-point Times Roman, on heavy bond paper. This was a sink-or-swim situation, and my colleagues just assumed I knew how to swim. "Just ask if you have a question," people told me, and I did—practically inhaling acronyms, policies, names, and procedures. As I had expected, it was an extremely intense place to work. But it was also surprisingly friendly. I soon learned that everybody from the chief of staff on down was on a first-name basis. The President was to be addressed as Mr. President, or sir.

I met him my second week on the job, just outside "the Oval"—staff lingo for the Oval Office. I was still a little bleary-eyed, having stayed up late the night before to finish my first solo assignment: his weekly radio address to the nation, on the AIDS crisis in Africa.

"Sir, this is your new speechwriter, John Pollack," said the communications director, Loretta Ucelli, wearing a pink dress that matched the walls of her West Wing office.

"Good to meet you," the President said, stepping forward to shake my hand.

"Thank you, sir," I answered.

"Nice bow tie!" he added, noting my yellow silk tie. Turning to the small group of staff, he took a quick poll. "Isn't that a great tie?" The others nodded in silent assent—nobody seemed inclined to dispute the most powerful man on earth.

In a small entourage, we proceeded to the ground floor of the Residence, where a crew had set up taping equipment in the Map Room. I stole a glance at the old, yellowing map on the wall, the one that gave the room its name. It was the last World War II battle map prepared for FDR before he died, in April of 1945. Although the room was now furnished with fine antiques and a large Oriental carpet, during the war it had served as the White House Situation Room. Clinton read the radio address perfectly, in one take. And then he was off to his waiting motorcade. I had survived.

At home that night, exhausted, I worked my way through the e-mail that had piled up over the week. Chris Sipola, at Cork Supply USA, hadn't heard from me in nearly a month and wanted a status update on the boat—including drawings. I sent him an apologetic e-mail, describing my new job and the demands it made on my time. I'm still committed to building the cork boat, I reassured him, but will have to postpone construction. I didn't, however, respond to his query about the drawings; there weren't any.

Over the next several months I found my rhythm, writing (and rewriting) one speech after the other, from radio addresses to policy speeches to eulogies to sharp commentaries on issues before Congress. Even as the world seemed to be heading downhill—flames of conflict in the Middle East, the attack on the USS *Cole,* the crash of Missouri governor Mel Carnahan's campaign plane—the White House still seemed full of hope and possibility. If the job demanded that I sacrifice almost every waking hour, if it meant getting woken up in the middle of the night, I didn't mind at all. I loved the job because I was back in the fray again, but this time at the very epicenter of American politics. And I was willing to give it every last ounce of my energy.

Or almost every ounce. Although my frequent morning-to-midnight schedule had forced me, or allowed me, to abandon most of my cork routes, I continued to collect from the few places that still called for pickup. "We've got corks everywhere!" one frustrated restaurant manager complained to my answering machine. "If you can't pick them up by tomorrow night, we're going to throw them out." Still dressed in a suit and tie, I would head back out the door for a midnight cork run, catching the last shift of waiters and busboys at the bar settling up on tips.

My friend Jan Vulevich, nicknamed the "Alabama Belle" for her captivating Southern charm, kept the corks coming, too. On her own initiative, she had sweet-talked several recalcitrant bartenders into saving corks by the bushel. Even her boss, the ABC commentator Cokie Roberts, started setting aside corks for the boat. "You are going to name that boat after me, aren't you?" the Alabama Belle would ask me with a sly smile, after every delivery. It wasn't quite a question.

"We'll see," I always answered, laughing. "Keep saving."

While juggling my various responsibilities to cork and country was exhausting, I had a little extra spring in my step everywhere I went. Because apart from the professional satisfaction I took from my job, I loved the texture of it all. I loved seeing how the Presidency worked from the inside, in its everyday detail.

A couple of months into the job, I was assigned to write a speech the President would deliver in Flint, Michigan. It was a plum assignment, because it meant a trip on *Air Force One*. As usual, I poured everything I had into that speech, which focused on bridging the digital divide for people with disabilities. When the big day arrived, I took an early-morning staff van out to Andrews Air Force Base and boarded the Presidential 747, to wait for his arrival.

After being shown to my assigned seat in the main cabin, which was arranged not in rows but as a lounge, I decided to take a look around. Making my way forward, past Air Force personnel and a few policy aides poring over thick briefing papers, I soon wandered into an empty suite up front before realizing that it was the President's.

I cast a nervous glance over my shoulder, but nobody seemed to have noticed me. And as long as I was already here, it couldn't hurt to take a quick look around, could it? At first glance, the office and adjacent bedroom, visible through a doorway, were larger than my whole apartment, and nicer, too. Emboldened, I stepped forward—only to be startled by a sharp electronic alarm that sent adrenaline jolting through me. Had I tripped a security beam?

No, it was only my pager. "Eagle Departs," the message said. That meant the President had lifted off from the South Lawn aboard *Marine One,* the Presidential helicopter, and was heading toward Andrews. I made a hasty exit, and returned to my own leather seat, with its armrest telephone and generous fruit basket.

Once the President was on board, the plane began racing down the runway without a moment's delay. I noticed right away that traditional seat-belt regulations didn't apply on *Air Force One,* or at least weren't enforced. Although I was buckled in, a couple of senior aides, regulars on the plane, remained standing as we hurtled into the air.

Just as I was settling in to enjoy the flight, one of the more influential aides approached to inform me that the President's speech needed a new passage. So much for kicking back on the flight of a lifetime. Michigan is only a short hop from Washington, especially when your plane doesn't have to compete with other aircraft for airspace or a gate assignment. I would have to work fast. Nerves a-jangle now, I headed for the small onboard office toward the rear. Taking a seat before its computer screen, I strapped myself in moments before the plane started to buck. Turbulence—just what I needed to settle my stomach. I picked up the phone, which had no keypad. Immediately, I was greeted by a White House operator. "What number, please?"

Moments later, Mara Silver, Terry's assistant, picked up back in the West Wing. I explained the information I needed. Could she find it and fax it to the plane?

While I waited, I decided to call my dad. Officially, personal calls were frowned upon. But I couldn't resist. How many other chances would I get to call him from *Air Force One*? I picked up the phone and gave his office number to the operator. The call went through instantly.

Voice mail. Damn! I left a message. And then, the fax whirring to life, it was time to get to work. The short flight passed in a flash of furious typing, and the revised speech emerged from the printer just as the plane's wheels screeched down onto the tarmac. With the plane taxiing, I grabbed the speech and hurried forward to the President's cabin. I knew right where it was.

Later, I stood in the back of a packed gymnasium, listening to the speech and waiting, nervously, for the audience reaction. I had hoped for a thunderous ovation, but what I witnessed was a different kind of affirmation: hundreds of deaf people fluttering their hands overhead—sign language for applause.

As exciting as days like that one were, I also appreciated the quieter, calmer moments at the White House. If I didn't have a speech due the next day, I used my "all access" blue badge to attend ceremonies in the Rose Garden, visit the White House chef in the basement of the Residence, or search out the Presidential calligraphers, who worked in a cramped East Wing studio penning fancy invitations to state dinners and other White House events.

Most days, no matter how busy I was, I ate lunch at the White House Mess. The Mess, run by the U.S. Navy, is a small, paneled dining room just across the corridor from the White House Situation Room. Although I took advantage of its takeout window when I was in a time crunch, I usually took a seat at the round staff table by the door.

With its heavy china and nice table linens, the Mess had a certain aura of tradition and ceremony about it, and the staff table drew an eclectic mix, from frazzled economic policy wonks to the perfectly coifed women of the White House Social Office. And if I managed to snag a seat against the wall, I could also keep an eye on the rest of the dining room, which was usually filled with cabinet secretaries, the occasional movie star, or visiting military brass. Although the food was good, this show alone was worth the price of lunch—usually about twelve bucks—and I really ate it up.

Often, after lunch, I would pause outside the Mess to appreciate the detailed scale model of the USS *Constitution,* which was on display in a large showcase. Launched in 1797 and still afloat today, "Old Ironsides" earned its nickname after a British cannonball bounced off its oaken hull in the War of 1812. The model was extraordinarily detailed, from its keel to its cannon to its complex rigging. The *Constitution*'s copper dinner gong—a relic of the days when the ship's hungry crew fought Barbary pirates and British frigates with equal abandon—rested in an adjacent case. Both spoke to my sense of history and adventure, hinting to me of the possibilities inherent in my own little boat.

Pretty soon, after word leaked about my project, several of the Navy stewards started saving corks for the boat, too.

ADRIFT

My time at the White House passed too quickly. The 2000 election came and stayed, and stayed, and finally ended a month later in what I considered outright robbery. The day the Supreme Court voted 5–4 to stop the Florida recount, handing Bush the Oval Office, I helped draft the President's response and faxed it, from the Situation Room, to his hotel in England.

Several interminable hours later, the four-page document came back, via the Situation Room, covered from start to finish with the President's hard-to-read scrawl. On reading through his extensive edits, my fellow speechwriters and I realized, to our dismay, that only three of our words had survived—*Vice President Gore.* The long fight was over.

A few weeks later, at a melancholy going-away party in the Press Office, I pocketed the last of my White House corks. But I didn't feel like celebrating. In the basement printshop of the chaotic OEOB, I noticed the staff already running tests on the new Bush auto-pen signature.

As darkness fell on January 19th, I packed the last of my things into a cardboard box, turned in my blue badge, and walked out the front gate of the White House onto the wet, glistening pavement of Pennsylvania Avenue. The bleachers outside, set up for Bush's inaugural parade, reminded me of gallows.

The next morning, I skipped the send-off rally for the Clintons at Andrews Air Force Base. Instead, I joined the protesters twenty deep along Pennsylvania Avenue, standing in the cold drizzle, furious and feeling like democracy had been raped. The press, which seemed to me so docile and complicit in Bush's coup-de-chad, largely ignored us. It was a miserable day.

Coming down with a fever, I stayed in my apartment for the next week, sick and depressed. I knew I had to get going again, to pick up my projects, to move on. But I didn't feel like it. When I finally forced myself to hit the streets collecting corks, I found that the routes had dried up. Except for the bartenders and waiters at the two or three places I had kept visiting on my late-night rounds, people had quit saving.

I was in a sour mood. When my conservative Italian barber, who always gave me a handful of corks from his mother-in-law, started ripping on Clinton one afternoon, I snapped back, "At least he didn't steal an election—I thought that only happened in Third World countries!" He went apoplectic, sputtering in anger. I got up from the chair and walked out.

Depressed and lacking all motivation to look for work, I

started channeling my frustration into cork assembly, spending hours banding them together into hexagonal units. It was mind-numbingly dull, but it did pass the time. As the hours turned into days and then to weeks, I lost steam. And with Garth still too busy to help much, half of me started asking: Do I really want to build this damned boat? And the other half answered: What the hell else do I have going?

The answer was nothing. My motivation was zilch. A half-hearted job search was leading nowhere. At the same time, my studio apartment was beginning to feel like a cell. I was tripping over corks. Somehow, I had become a prisoner of my own so-called freedom.

Finally, I called my mom and poured out my woes. I told her I was going nowhere fast; that the cork boat felt like an albatross around my neck; that I was frustrated with Garth; and that I wanted to quit. "Who the hell cares if I build a fucking cork boat, anyway!"

My mom listened patiently. And then she spoke. "I know you're frustrated. But look, you've been talking about the boat since you were a little boy. You've come too far on it to give up now. Just don't worry about Garth. If you have to do this without him, you will. You're an organizer. The boat is an organizing project. So organize."

She knew my talents in this arena firsthand, and those skills were the same whether it meant recruiting and training volunteers for a get-out-the-vote effort or building an unconventional boat.

"I know," I said. "But—"

She cut me off. "John, you have the capacity to inspire people and to bring them to your cause. Just get out there and recruit people. They'll help you build the boat. I know you can do it. But if you give up now, you'll always regret it."

Although I wasn't always eager to accept my mom's frequent advice, I knew she was right this time. I *had* come too far. I had to go forward. After hanging up the phone, I decided that I would make construction of the cork boat my one and only goal for the year. If I only got one thing accomplished, if I drained my savings account down to zero, if I went stark raving mad in the process, I would get that damned boat built and into the water.

My first recruit was Jock Friedly, a gregarious friend from college whose small dot-com, after more than a million dollars in venture capital and a year of furious effort, had all but gone under. With a lot of spare time suddenly at his disposal, Jock seemed willing, even eager, to pitch in.

Assembling corks at my kitchen table was mindless work, but in fits and starts we made some steady progress. Steady but slow. Real progress would depend on a large-scale volunteer effort, which required finding a real workshop, and soon.

And then Garth found one, sort of, in his new group house, a place called the Lamont Street Collective. Located in Mount Pleasant, a couple of neighborhoods north of Dupont

Circle, the Collective was a quintessential Washington co-op: a three-story 1920s row house with an old, damp couch on the porch, a foyer crowded with mountain bikes, and a big magazine rack filled with back issues of *The Nation, Mother Jones,* and *National Geographic.* Sitting in the kitchen with Garth on my first visit, I looked up at the ceiling, and saw rotting slats through a hole in the crumbling plaster.

Garth followed my gaze. "Oh. There's a bathtub right there," he said.

I shifted my chair to the side.

"Don't worry," he deadpanned. "Nobody's *in* it."

We broke up laughing. Yes, the Lamont Street Collective was a little run-down, but it had a lot of character. In fact, the whole neighborhood did. It was one of the few integrated areas in Washington—a mix of working-class African-Americans, recent Hispanic immigrants, and the mostly white, nonprofit Birkenstock crowd who lived in places like the Lamont Street Collective. But it was starting to gentrify, and while the granola-crunchers took pride in local diversity, some longtime residents were getting priced out.

Still, there was a strong sense of community, and if Garth was happy there, so was I. Especially since his new housemates had told him we could use one of the basement storage rooms for the cork boat project. All we had to do was clear out the junk inside.

And so we did, hauling away dusty fans, a broken weight bench, musty furniture, vinyl suitcases, and a crumpled brown bag of rusting campaign buttons for Frank Zeidler, the Socialist Party candidate for President in 1976. But after we hauled in all our sacks of corks, there really wasn't much room left for construction. If we actually built the boat down there, how would we ever get it out? But I kept these worries to myself. It was better than nothing, and at least it got fifty thousand corks out of our way. Besides, Garth already had his eye on the two-car garage out back.

A few weeks later, over dinner, we laid out our boat plans for the coming months. If we were serious about getting our craft in the water over the summer, we were going to need a huge shipment of corks from Cork Supply USA to supplement those I had collected locally. And we needed to figure out a way to speed up disk assembly. The rubber bands helped enormously, but the assembly process still took too long. On a napkin, Garth sketched out a potential solution: a hexagonal jig—a tray, really—cut to hold precisely one disk's worth of corks.

"A template would let us go a lot faster," he said. "All we'd have to do is fill it up."

Having spent the past couple of weeks assembling disks cork by cork, I was all for time-saving innovation. And after a few days of experimentation, we settled on a standard disk size: hexagonal disk about 14 inches in diameter, consisting of precisely 127 corks. This was no random number. For buoyancy's sake, our disks had to be big enough in diameter that—once stacked—they would form a uniform log of some heft.

At the same time, they couldn't be too big around, or their circumference would exceed the width of the commercial fishnet in which we planned to sheathe them.

Snagging a few sheets of stiff, lightweight foam-core that his office used to build architectural models, Garth assembled a template. Together, we gave it a try. It was, as I wrote in my journal, revolutionary. This new standardized disk-assembly method slashed construction time by at least seventy-five percent; what had taken about twelve minutes, we could now accomplish in three. All we had to do was fill a template with corks, stretch one of our long 117-B's around the perimeter, carefully remove the assembly, and voilà—we had a disk.

It was a radical breakthrough and, better yet, as scalable as Henry Ford's Model T assembly line. So what if putting the band on improperly caused the disk to explode like a cork volcano? We'd get the hang of it. And as Garth said, the cell-like array we had just created was somewhat analogous to the cell structure of the cork itself. In short, our approach made sense, or at least as much sense as any cork boat could make.

Fired up now, we decided to contact Cork Supply USA immediately, to see about getting corks in bulk. After an exchange of e-mails, Chris Sipola, sounding a little dubious after my six-month hiatus, agreed to ship us a load of the company's rejects: corks that had fallen on the floor of the factory, been misprinted, or failed quality control. All we would have to pay for was the estimated $2,000 to truck them from California, he said.

I swallowed hard. Two grand? I was unemployed. Garth, underpaid in architecture, was moonlighting as a Web designer to make ends meet, but still scrambled for rent money and the cash to pay his frequent parking tickets. So much for all those "free" corks, I thought to myself, torn between gratitude and total discouragement. I thanked Chris, and said I would investigate a cheaper way to ship. The answer turned out to be Amtrak. The cost: $682.

It was more than either Garth or I wanted to spend, but as I told him: "We can't just talk this boat into existence. We have to build it, and that's going to mean laying out some cash now and then. Boats are expensive, even 'free' ones." We agreed to split the cost.

A few weeks later, when the call came in from the freight dock at Union Station, Garth and I rented a large U-Haul truck and drove down to pick up our shipment. The freight dock at Union Station was a drab utilitarian affair, a boxy industrial cavern that was empty save for a big freight scale and a cramped office behind a dirty glass window. One of the beefy freight handlers, impatient with my repeated clumsy attempts to back the truck up to the loading dock through honking, rush-hour traffic, relieved me of my post at the

wheel with no small degree of disgust. But when I mentioned what we were picking up and why, his attitude changed
entirely.

"You're building what?" he asked, incredulous.

"A boat, out of wine corks," I said. "It's going to be the
world's first cork boat!"

"Why?"

"For fun."

He loved it. Although he confessed that his tastes ran more
to six-packs and jet-skis, he thought the project was cool.

While I signed the necessary documents in triplicate inside
the little office, our new friend returned atop a big yellow
forklift bearing a huge, shrink-wrapped pallet. "This is just
one of them," he said. With an easy, technical grace, he slid the
pallet neatly into the back of the truck and shoved it forward.
After fetching two more loads with the fork, he climbed down
and insisted on shaking our hands. "Good luck, you guys! Let
me know how it goes."

We thanked him, snapped a few photos for posterity, and
rumbled off in our laden U-Haul, back toward the Lamont
Street Collective, where, somehow, in a diplomatic coup of
historic persuasiveness, Garth had convinced his new housemates to sacrifice their garage for the boat. Street parking was
in chronic short supply, but the cork boat, Garth argued,
was an environmentally sensitive project, a statement against
nonrenewable plastic corks and a small blow against Big Oil.

"Besides," he said, "it's only for a couple of months." That—
and the promise of fifty dollars a month in rent—had done
the trick.

When we pulled into the alley with our bounty of corks, I
wasn't quite sure what to expect. I had seen the garage briefly,
at night, with cars in it. Daylight didn't improve the picture
much. Small and cramped, it was pretty depressing by any
standard—a dimly lit concrete bunker with a cracked slab
ceiling, a greasy floor, and walls smudged black with exhaust
fumes. But it was big enough to build the boat, and it was
all ours.

"Way to go, brother!" I told Garth, genuinely excited. "It's
great!"

Without a forklift to unload the pallets, we had to cut away
the shrink-wrap and drag out the heavy burlap sacks of loose
cork, one by one. Stacked up in a corner like giant, heavy
beanbags, they took up nearly a quarter of the garage and rose
almost to the ceiling. Sweating despite the damp chill, I
looked at my watch. In just over three hours, we had bumped
our cork total from fifty thousand to a staggering quarter-
million. There was no turning back now.

As storm clouds gathered, we closed the garage doors and
rumbled off to return the truck to the U-Haul facility. Located,
appropriately, along a grim stretch of U Street, the office consisted of a gray shipping container set behind a fence topped
with coiled razor-wire. What a surprise—it was closed. When

we had picked the truck up, the sullen twenty-something attendant had snapped at Garth for blocking her view of the TV. She had probably left early.

Following instructions on a sign at the gate, we parked the truck in the dirt lot next door, which was strewn with cardboard boxes, scraps of rotting plywood, and a shattered toilet. Relieved to be done with the vehicle, I dropped its keys into a designated drop-box and we headed for Garth's car. Spotting us, a man in a dirty windbreaker approached quickly from across the street, blocking our path. His rheumy eyes had a nasty gleam, and he reached into a crumpled black bag. Half expecting a gun, I was almost relieved to see him proffer a handful of raunchy porn videos.

"No thanks," I said firmly, as we shoved past him, on either side. We were just two guys trying to build a cork boat, and pornography wasn't on our agenda. The sudden juxtaposition of our respective ventures, though, was a little jarring. I felt extremely fortunate to be living my life, not his.

That night, it rained. The garage's cracked roof leaked like a sieve, soaking everything. I told Garth it was a good thing we were building a boat, because boats were supposed to get wet. It would take more than a downpour to dampen our spirits.

SUMMER STORMS

As cold spring rains gradually gave way to a muggy summer, that garage became something of a second home. We had cleaned it up a bit, caulking the leaky roof as best we could, and laying down sheets of Masonite over the worst of the grease. Except for the flies and mosquitoes, which came out at different times of day, it turned out to be a pretty good workshop. We dubbed it the Mount Pleasant Boat Works.

Ever the organizer, I approached the whole project like Tom Sawyer with a fence to paint. The work was inherently dull, but I tried to make it sound like a party, and a party with a mission. "Listen, I have an opportunity for you," I'd say, calling early in the week so people couldn't claim they already had weekend plans. "We're building the world's first cork boat, and I need your help. What are you doing Saturday?" If they said they were busy, I hit them with Sunday. It was sort of a trap, but I needed the bodies. And I knew they would have a pretty good time.

Before long—if I was aggressive in my calls—I could get

six or eight people working on the boat most weekend afternoons. And with the radio on, some beer, and a jug of lemonade to make the afternoon pass easily, it turned into a regular party. Pretty soon, a few people were calling me mid-week: "Are we doing corks this weekend?" Some were former White House colleagues like Heather Hurlburt and Mara Silver. Others I knew from social circles, such as Michele Rivard, who had been on board since that first day with the glue guns, and the ever-present, indefatigable Jock Friedly. It was a cerebral bunch, but they were eager to work with their hands.

The main task, before banding corks into disks, was sorting out good corks from bad. Not only were the used, locally collected corks of varied quality, but the mammoth shipment from Cork Supply USA had also turned out to be a mixed blessing, literally. Roughly half were perfect, but nearly half were the agglomerates, which soaked up a lot of water. They came out of the big burlap sacks all jumbled together, and we had to take a close look at each and every one to tell the difference. Build a boat of agglomerates, and we might as well build a cork submarine.

As easygoing as he was, Jock took this cork sorting very seriously. And in examining literally tens of thousands of corks, he came to know his corks well. A stickler for quality control, he became the unofficial trainer of new volunteers. "This one is a bad one," he would explain, holding up an agglomerate for newcomers to examine. "It has disks of solid cork on either end, but don't be fooled. If you look closely, the middle is made up of bits and pieces. They soak up water. We toss them."

Most people caught on quickly; those with rare natural talent learned to tell the difference merely by a cork's weight, without even looking. Sorting so many corks, we also came to know and appreciate a great number of different vineyards—not for the quality of their wine, but for the quality of their corks.

"Every one smells different, looks different, and feels different," said Garth, who loved corks for their infinite variety, and occasionally rubbed one across his lips, just for the feel of it. "The irony is that we need uniformity."

In addition to their quality, we also started judging them for their logos. Most were either dull or tried too hard with their pretentious, heraldic crests. Others were more clever. We tossed the most interesting ones into a drawer Garth had labeled "The Museum."

One of the best was a series from an inexpensive wine called Reds. These corks featured iconic images including Nikita Khrushchev banging his shoe at the United Nations, Karl Marx smoking a cigar, the bearded Vladimir Lenin, and Senator Joe McCarthy. The wine's slogan was "A Wine for the People," and we tried to collect them all.

Other corks had compelling graphics—a flying goose, a growling wolf, or a falling leaf. Still others boasted a catchy word or phrase, such as "Taste a Dream," "Drink Naked," "Prosperity," or the nonsensical, down-to-earth "Ribbit!" One of my favorites was a lone cork from Justin Vineyards & Winery, on California's rugged central coast. It featured an entire political treatise in a tiny typeface, reading:

JUST A PUNCH

JUST A DIMPLE

JUST A CHAD

JUST A PREGNANT CHAD

JUST COUNT

JUST RECOUNT

JUST APPEAL

JUST REAPPEAL

JUST DECIDE

JUST CALL 1-800-726-0049

I liked the cork because it mixed politics and puns. Other volunteers had their own favorites, and we encouraged them to take samples.

Corks aside, sorting and "disking" was mindless work that left a lot of room for good conversation. The topics changed

as new people came and went, ranging from classical music to Egyptian water policy to Latino politics in Los Angeles. A fairly literate crew, we also discussed books we were reading, or shared new words we had just learned. One of my favorite new words was *tessellation:* the "careful juxtaposition of elements into a coherent pattern," as in a mosaic. Our corks, in strict hexagonal order, were a perfect example of tessellation. In my dictionary, the word was also a close (though linguistically unrelated) neighbor of the word *tessaraconter,* a galley ship with forty banks of oars. Our boat would be considerably smaller, but the idea was essentially the same.

We also spent considerable time testing out different names for the boat. Although Garth and I had initially picked the alliterative *Cork Cutter,* we had abandoned that in hopes of coming up with something more compelling. When Brandt forwarded a Word-A-Day e-mail introducing me to the adjective *suberic* (of or pertaining to cork), we threw that into the mix of possibilities. Ultimately, though, it was too close to *submarine,* and we abandoned that name, too. Finally, Garth asked why we didn't just give it the name that people were already effectively using—*Cork Boat*?

"It's so postmodern, it's great," he said.

I didn't have a clue about postmodernism, but the name fit. *Cork Boat* it was.

As social as the Boat Works had become, I wasn't always relaxed when I was there. On the surface, perhaps, but not deep down. I was responsible for running the show, and I could see the weeks passing. I could calculate the work ahead. And though I often worked in the Boat Works alone for long hours during the week, trying to speed things along, I was growing more and more anxious about the schedule. At the rate we were going, a fall launch was going to be tight.

It was about this time that a friend of mine, a geophysics professor at Penn State, e-mailed to ask if I would be interested in joining a research expedition he was organizing to Antarctica, in November and December. He wanted me to be the team's designated writer, filing dispatches and drumming up press. The expedition wouldn't pay, but that didn't bother me. Given my current employment status, the financial impact of two months in Antarctica would be nil. How could I pass up such a grand adventure? I e-mailed back a solid yes.

Surely, the boat would be done before I flew south for the winter—or summer, as it would be in the Southern Hemisphere. I would make it happen. I would just need to find more volunteers to speed up the process. Volunteer recruitment, like cork collection, fell mostly on me, and I was constantly on the lookout. Meeting new people, I'd sound them out about volunteering for the boat at the first polite opportunity.

Usually, this came within minutes of introduction. This was because in Washington, the first question after meeting someone is usually: "What do you do?" On one level, it's a benign conversation starter. On another, it's a quick gauge of a person's place on the totem pole of power. The question had always irked me, even when I worked at the White House. But not now. With the boat under construction, I was happy to answer: "I'm building a cork boat."

"You're what?" came the inevitable reply.

"A Viking ship made entirely of wine corks—and you can help build it," I would answer, inviting them out to the garage. Some people thought I was crazy—and told me so. Others said, "Just call me for the launch." Still others actually showed up. A few became regulars. I'd even lasso passersby walking past the open garage doors with a pitch to join us, and one or two became star volunteers.

The garage, like all of its neighbors, opened onto the central alley that ran between houses down the middle of the block. That alley, with its trash cans and junked cars and comings and goings, had a pulse and culture all its own. There was the big lady with the enormous square jaw and a speech impediment who always walked past at about ten A.M., with a friendly "Hiya, buddy!" There was Mac, the old taxi driver, who came and went as calls came in—always casting a skeptical look my way—as his station wagon leaked oil like the *Exxon Valdez*. And then there was Joe, the cheerful former cop who had every tool known to man and was eager to loan them. "If I weren't married, I'd join you guys in a heartbeat," he would say, a little wistfully, as family duties inevitably took him back up the alley to his house. We also came to know the neighbor boys, seven-year-old Walter and his little brother, Ezra, who would pedal up on their bikes to check on the boat's progress, and help us out by sorting corks.

The neighbor I saw most often, though, was Harold Wilson, a contractor who rented the basement apartment in a run-down house directly across the alley, and who stopped by to chat at least once a day. Approaching sixty now, he had built his own share of boats as a young man, he said, including a racing catamaran in Vancouver that had been outlawed by the harbor patrol for being too fast. At first he seemed a little dubious about this would-be cork boat, which, admittedly, was still in hundreds of thousands of pieces. He was also a little dubious about us.

"Only two rich white boys would do something like this," he said, shaking his head. Harold was black, and often made wry comments about race. "You have too much time and money on your hands." But as the months passed, and the sacks of loose corks started giving way to neat stacks of hexagonal disks, he grew more and more intrigued by the project, loaning us tools, advice, and the occasional helping hand. "I think you'll make it," he told me one day. "I thought you were crazy, but you'll make it."

I was starting to think so, too. And then one hot afternoon we finally finished rubber-banding the first log, a twelve-foot column of ninety-six identical disks. It was extraordinary to behold: exactly 12,192 corks held in precise order by 824 rubber bands—and not a drop of glue. Garth and I were both a little stunned by our own creation, a cork Column of Trajan that in all its remarkable, diminutive detail told our own tale of ambition, sweat, toil, and glory.

It was almost a month before we solved the next challenge: how to give the log rigidity. I was all for the quick solution, which was to sew a net sheath around the log as it was. Garth insisted that we had to strengthen it somehow first. "We need to put the log into compression," he said, to compress it along its longitudinal axis. He was the architect and absolutely certain on this point, so I deferred.

Together we sketched out possibilities, and settled on a plan. We would sew matching net "hoods" over the ends of each log, encircled by Dacron loops we called "collars." Tying six separate lines to one of the collars—one line along each face of the hexagonal log—we would run them through the opposite collar, then loop back again. Theoretically, at least, we could compress the whole log by tightening the lines.

I spent the next several days tracking down the right kind of line, and learning to sew on the net hoods. It wasn't easy. The netting was designed to catch fish, not cork. Garth, overwhelmed by his job and a massive freelance website project, checked in periodically. "The coder keeps fucking everything up!" he complained, alluding to his absence.

In turn, I complained to Jock. "Am I expecting too much from Garth?" I asked.

"You two just have different work styles," he said. "My own style is closer to his. I tend to work much more effectively when I have a fire lit under me. Yours is going to be more effective in getting the boat done."

Still, I fumed all week. And so, apparently, did Garth. When he finally showed up at the Boat Works that Saturday, we could hardly speak to each other. I was angry to be doing so much scut work alone. Meanwhile, Garth was frustrated to see the project moving ahead without him.

After a sullen half-hour or so, we talked it out. We didn't really resolve anything, but at least we were able to channel our tension into the task at hand. We had to, because compressing our first log was definitely a job for two people. We had to tighten the lines slowly and evenly on opposite faces of the log, and do it simultaneously. Otherwise, the log might suddenly bow in one direction, exploding in a shower of corks. With the log flat on the floor, we donned rubber gloves to protect our hands from rope burn and tightened those lines until they hummed like a string bass. The system Garth had conceived worked perfectly. All that remained undone was to sew on a net sheath, and the log would be complete and ready for use.

Breakthroughs like this always helped restore our sense of camaraderie, and we celebrated over dinner at the long table in the co-op's dining room. The table, built of surplus planking from the Washington Navy Yard, was always open to friends of friends, and Garth was particularly hospitable, even when we were having our differences. One of Garth's housemates, who rarely ventured down the back steps to the Boat Works unless he was taking out the trash, asked us about our progress. Apparently, he had bet a case of champagne that we would never finish.

We were ecstatic to report that the first cork log—the basic building block of our boat—was no longer theory, but reality.

But there was another reality, too. I had all but spent my federal tax refund, and needed to make some money. I wasn't exactly desperate yet, but pretty soon I would have to suck it up and find work.

Fortunately, as things turned out, a job found me just a few days later, when Congressman Bonior's communications director called. Prefacing her remarks with "I know this is a long shot, but . . . ," she told me that my successor had quit and Bonior was desperate for a speechwriter. "I don't suppose you'd be willing to come back half-time, until the end of the year?" she asked.

I was torn. The thought of returning to work for my old boss felt like a step backward, professionally. I had fled the Hill, swearing never to return. I had since written for one of modern America's great orators. And I wasn't too psyched about returning to the bloody trenches of Congress for the daily diatribe against the GOP, however much I felt they probably deserved it.

But I needed a job, and the deal offered was a great one: half-time, at my old salary, with benefits. After thinking about it for a few days, I agreed. But I made it very clear that I would continue to build the boat, and might need time off, in the crunch, to finish it. Also, I said I could only work through

October; I would be heading to Antarctica for the rest of the year.

It was a deal. The next week, I put on a suit and tie, swallowed my pride, and returned to the Capitol. "Hey, long time no see," the elevator operator said when she saw me. "How's the boat? I've got some corks for you!" I told her the boat was coming along, and that we were launching on Columbus Day. And, yes, I still needed her corks.

Sitting down at my old, ugly desk a few minutes later, my first day back, I opened the upper file drawer. My heart sank. All my disorganized files were still there, exactly as I'd left them a year and a half earlier. It was as if I'd never left. Still, I needed the work and, as I kept reminding myself, it wasn't permanent.

The truth is, I soon discovered that working two or three days a week was just fine; in fact, I liked it. The job gave my week structure, alleviated some of my loneliness, and relieved the money crunch, while still affording me time to work on the boat. I also had ready access to a new pool of recruits and, with time to proselytize, soon had a crew of friends from the office out at the Boat Works on weekends, assembling corks. But even with my new volunteers, I knew it was going to be tough finishing the boat by October. Sorting corks and building the logs took time, and we had yet to figure out how to lash them together. There wasn't much I could do, though, to speed things up.

One sweltering Saturday, with the temperature in the nineties and the garage a muggy oven, Garth, a half-dozen volunteers, and I were slogging away, assembling corks. It was so hot that even the flies were quiet. Despite the heat, our mood was upbeat; we were knocking it out, a team in action. Always conscious of morale, I talked of the glorious river trip we would all take when it was finished, floating past crumbling castles and plucking clusters of plump, juicy grapes from the riverbanks. I didn't know how many people would fit on the boat, I said, but we'd just have to build it big enough.

And then a friend of Garth's wandered into the Boat Works, a buddy from out of town who had surprised him with a visit. My first thought was: Great, another set of hands. But one quick look at all of us and this fellow apparently had a better idea. "Hey, Garth, let's go climbing," he said.

Conversation stopped. I felt as if a hammer had struck a mirror and shards of glass were falling to the concrete floor. It only took an instant: Garth looked at me. I looked at him. Garth looked at his buddy. Here were all these volunteers, sacrificing their Saturday afternoon to help build a cork boat that, despite all my talk of romantic rivers and French grapes, was probably never going to carry them farther than a ride on the Potomac. I could tell he was torn but, in my mind, this was a moment of truth.

"I'll be back in a few hours," Garth said. He walked out.

I was so furious that I was beyond words. A long minute passed. "Lemonade, anyone?" I asked, struggling to feign normalcy. We kept on working, cork by cork, through the heat. I hoped nobody noticed the tension.

All the volunteers were gone by the time Garth got back. Right away, I lit in with a vengeance. "It would have been better if you had never shown up today in the first place. Do you know how hard I work to get people in here, into your garage, building what is supposedly *your* fucking boat? Don't you think they have something they'd rather do, too? Don't you think they'd like to be somewhere else on a Saturday afternoon besides this hot, shitty garage, sorting corks?"

Defensive, Garth counterattacked. His friend was going through a tough time, and had needed to talk. Besides, why did the boat always move ahead on my schedule? And just why, exactly, did the boat have to launch in the fall? A Columbus Day launch was totally unrealistic, he said. "I've done a lot more projects than you, and you don't know how much time it takes," he said. "We don't even have a real design."

"Then start designing!" I shouted. "The difference between us is this: I see a great cork boat in the water this fall. You see a perfect boat, sometime in the future. And on your schedule, that future is never. You can help or not, but there *will* be a boat in the water on Columbus Day."

The truth was, Garth did have more experience building things. I knew that he could contribute a lot more to the project if he would just stop being so stubborn and kick into gear. But at the same time, there was something holding him back.

It wasn't just his priorities, which were apparently different from mine, or the fact that he always felt strapped for cash. It was something deeper. He was not just a procrastinator, but a perfectionist. To actually build a real boat meant building something that was, by virtue of existing, necessarily imperfect. Was he unconsciously putting off building that imperfect boat forever?

For my part, I couldn't let the boat project slip for yet another season. If the project lost momentum now, it really would be lost forever. I wouldn't let that happen. Not after saving corks my entire life. Not after so much work. Not after staking my reputation on it. I was the cork guy, and I would finish that damned boat by October 7 if it killed me.

Could I do it without Garth? If I had to. I was the one who had come up with the original idea. I had collected the corks, found the sponsors, recruited the volunteers, and figured out much of the engineering. Yes, I desperately wanted Garth's full participation—his energy, his design talents, his hands-on building experience. Yes, we were supposedly in this fifty-fifty. But if he called my bluff I would finish the boat alone.

Garth, perhaps sensing my determination, perhaps just tired of fighting, or perhaps conceding that a fall launch was possible after all, finally agreed. We would launch over Columbus Day weekend. Though still angry, we settled down to plot out a final schedule. Our first deadline would be Labor Day, about a month away. We would have two logs completed by then and would get them into the water for a test. Garth said he'd talk with a friend who had a swimming pool. I said I'd line up transportation; hauling twelve-foot logs weighing several hundred pounds apiece would require an SUV. And

Garth, finally committing to tackle the project full-bore, said he'd take vacation time going into the home stretch.

"We're going to be pulling all-nighters," he warned.

Labor Day came, and our two cork logs splashed into the pool. We lashed them together with webbing, jumped into the water, and pulled ourselves aboard, cheering. The logs floated beautifully, even with two guys standing on them, jumping on them, and putting them through a workout.

As we cheered and splashed around the pool, an old friend from my days on Mackinac Island, Lawrence Sheets, taped it all for National Public Radio. In the seventeen years since we had first met, Lawrence had become a successful foreign correspondent in the former Soviet Union. Recently hired by NPR as their Moscow correspondent, he had come to Washington for training and orientation. And he'd sold them on a story about the "Cork Wars," with the *Cork Boat* as a quirky lead. Both Garth and I were NPR fanatics, and we were psyched about the publicity; a story on *All Things Considered* would be a major coup.

The swimming-pool test demonstrated the strength of our basic design. Although finishing the boat in less than six weeks would be a real ball-breaker, even Garth said we might just pull it off. September was going to be a fun month.

9/11

A week later, approaching the Capitol, I saw Bonior outside doing a stand-up—an interview—with one of the TV networks. As the Democratic Whip, he gave these interviews several times a week. I stopped to listen, glad for the excuse to linger for a few minutes in the morning sunshine. They were asking him about some pending legislation.

Steve, Bonior's plainclothes bodyguard, leaned over to me, pointing to the earpiece that coiled from his ear. "A plane just hit the World Trade Center," he whispered. A moment later, the reporter's cell phone rang. She got the news, too.

Concerned, we hurried inside the Capitol and up to the Whip's office, where several TVs showed the flames and the smoke billowing into the sky. Then we recoiled, suddenly, as another plane hit the second tower. Like the rest of America, we watched in horror, unable to quite comprehend what we were seeing, live on TV.

Then the anchor broke in, with news of smoke from the

Pentagon. Another plane had crashed there, and a fourth jet-liner was missing, presumably hijacked.

We looked at each other. "Steve," Bonior said. "Maybe we should evacuate."

"They're telling people to stay put," Steve answered, listening to his earpiece.

I stuck my head out the door, into the corridor. People were rushing for the exits in a quiet panic. "Gephardt's staff is going," I reported, shutting the door again. They were higher up the political food chain. Maybe they knew something we didn't. Still, I was inclined to stay inside. The Capitol is an old, massive building, built of block after block of solid stone. Its dome is really two domes, one inside the other, both of iron and supported with heavy truss-work. Our section had been rebuilt in the 1950s, at the height of the Cold War. But could it survive a direct hit?

Bonior, an Army veteran, made the decision. "Let's go," he said grimly. "Now."

We all dashed. The scene in the corridors had turned to chaos. People were running, falling, picking themselves up. We hurried down the marble steps, past the House Chamber, and down to the first floor. The Capitol Police were at the Members' Entrance, shouting and waving people through.

"Evacuate the building! Evacuate the building! There's a plane heading for the Capitol! Get Out!"

This is like a grade-B movie, I thought, running. I can't believe it's happening. And then we were suddenly outside, in the bright sunshine, and . . . nothing. No plane. Not even the sight of smoke from the Pentagon, just across the river. We gathered in clusters on the Capitol lawn. There were hundreds of people. Democrats and Republicans. Congressmen and pages. Cafeteria workers and police. What was going on? Nobody seemed to know, except that it seemed, somehow, we were at war.

After a few minutes, Steve hustled Bonior off to a waiting police van. House leadership were being taken to a "secret, secure location," probably a bunker somewhere in Virginia. The rest of us, rather than waiting at the Capitol for Armageddon, walked to a colleague's nearby apartment to call our families, watch the news, and wait out whatever was going to happen next.

That afternoon, after having watched the towers collapse over and over again, I walked home alone, across town. The Metro had been shut down, and the streets were strangely empty for a Tuesday. Passing in front of Union Station, I watched a somber park ranger lowering the flags of the fifty states to half-mast one by one, their rusty pulleys screeching in protest.

I choked up, thinking of all the losses in my own life—my grandparents, gone many years now; and my gruff, spirited mentor from my days in Madrid, Bill Montalbano, felled by a heart attack while walking to work. But mostly I grieved for Sara. After twenty-three years it still hurt.

The next day, when the Capitol reopened under heavy

security, it was a different, more sober place. I wrote as best I could: a brief floor speech for Bonior decrying the attacks, and a letter of condolence and gratitude from our office to the families of those passengers who'd brought down the fourth plane, in Pennsylvania. Had we been the intended target? We didn't know for sure, but felt incredibly lucky to have escaped the doom that killed so many others.

The rest of the week dragged by, the footage of carnage and rescue efforts and ceremonies blurring into one long nightmare. Members of Congress—at least in the Democratic caucus—shouted at each other behind closed doors, angry and powerless. But in a show of remarkable bipartisan unity, Congress opened the government coffers without reserve, by the billions. To me, government had never looked so rich, or so weak.

Saturday, a blessed respite, finally arrived. I drove over to the Boat Works, opened the garage doors, and stared at the detritus of a project I had pursued all my life. There were the big burlap sacks piled in the corner, bulging with the corks I had collected—somewhere in the neighborhood of seventy thousand by now—some spilling onto the floor. There were the two test logs that had floated so well. And the sacks of virgin corks, stacked to the ceiling, awaiting assembly. There were design sketches tacked to a corkboard, and a twelve-foot length of aluminum roof gutter—a failed attempt to fix the leaks overhead. Standing there, I struggled to gain some sort of perspective on this new world of terror.

When Garth came down the stairs a few minutes later, we embraced. After everything that had happened, our squabbles seemed just that—squabbles. We were friends first and foremost, and nothing else mattered. Not anymore.

Silent, manual work was just what we needed, and we started sorting corks. I hadn't had the heart to call any volunteers. I just didn't feel like pushing the project at a time when it seemed the whole world had been upended. After all, what did the *Cork Boat* matter in the wake of 9/11?

The roar of a low-flying jet cut through our thoughts. We stepped outside to search the sky. Another fighter, on patrol over the city, streaked overhead. Harold came out into the alley, too, looking up. I wondered aloud if maybe, given everything, we should just give the boat a rest for a few months. Nobody knew what to say.

The next morning, Sunday, I found myself back at the Boat Works again, assembling corks. Taking all these jumbled, small objects and fixing them in an orderly, hexagonal array felt good to me, as if, in some small way, I could create order from chaos.

Then Heather came walking up the alley. "I was hoping you'd be here," she said. She told me she needed to get her mind off the world, and sorting corks was just the medicine. Twenty minutes later, Katherine Switz stopped by looking for some "cork therapy." And then Jock Friedly, out for a run. And Michele Rivard. By day's end there were six or seven people in the garage, working with a quiet fury. It was a forced march toward normalcy, Osama bin Laden be damned. By the time I shut the garage doors at sunset, we had sorted and banded eighteen thousand corks, a new single-day record.

And I had made up my mind. In the wake of 9/11, the *Cork Boat* didn't matter less, it mattered more. In a world riven by hatred and suffused with danger, nurturing a sense of play and whimsy seemed all the more important, for reasons I couldn't quite articulate. No, I couldn't drop the project. Not now.

On Tuesday morning, Lloyd Grove of the *Washington Post* called. Grove was the gossip columnist whose "Reliable Source" was perhaps the best-read column in the paper. "I hear you're building a boat out of wine corks," he said. "I'd like to talk to you about that and get a photographer out there to get some pictures."

The photographer came that afternoon, but he didn't seem too interested in taking pictures. He talked and asked questions for twenty minutes, camera at his side. I realized afterward that it took him that long simply to figure out what to shoot, because there was no boat yet—not even anything remotely resembling a boat. But he had his assignment, and eventually found his shot.

The piece that came out was good. A CORKING GOOD VOYAGE, the headline said. I had been careful to explain that, while some people might think the project frivolous in light of recent events, the boat was all about whimsy. "Whimsy is all the more important in the world we live in now," I said, adding that *Cork Boat* volunteers also enjoyed a sense of camaraderie and community.

Grove had phoned John Podesta and asked him if he'd like to help build the boat. "I know John and he's a good guy," Podesta answered. "But I think I'll stick to giving blood."

As it turns out, people loved the piece—and the boat. In Michigan, a friend of the family saw my mom at a memorial service and told her that the story of the *Cork Boat* had sparked her first smile since 9/11. At work on the Hill, hundreds of corks poured in. Apparently, people had been saving them for years, just like I had, though perhaps without the same specificity of purpose.

My friend Ken Weine, the communications director at *Newsweek,* called from New York to offer congratulations. We had worked side by side on some tough, heartbreaking political campaigns, and we both knew how hard it was to get press, let alone good press. He was also a longtime skeptic when it came to the boat project.

"See what you've done?" he chided me. "Right now, there's some third-term congressman berating his poor press secretary, saying, 'I've been in Congress for five years, and you still haven't gotten me into the "Reliable Source." A boat! A boat! Why didn't *you* think of a lousy cork boat?' "

A few days later, I drove to Annapolis to search for an old wooden mast. Despite Garth's resistance—he was satisfied with oars—I insisted on a sail. "We're not building a rowboat," I told him.

Annapolis, less than an hour's drive but a world away from Washington, is a quaint eighteenth-century seaport and home to the United States Naval Academy. Rife with boatyards, the town was bound to have what I was looking for. But several phone calls had revealed that wooden masts were hard to find; traditional masts had given way to aluminum some forty years ago. Still, I just couldn't see putting an aluminum mast on the *Cork Boat;* the aesthetic would be all wrong.

At Bacon Sails, a sail and salvage house, a salesman led me back into the crowded warehouse to see what he had. The place was packed with hundreds upon hundreds of sails, aluminum spars, masts, rigging, outboard motors, inflatable rafts, rusting anchors, and one lone motorcycle. "There isn't going to be much choice," he warned, "but we'll figure something out."

And we did. Rummaging through a dusty rack, he turned up a spruce mast, boom, and matching sail, all for $300. It would be a little undersized for the boat I was describing, he said, but that was probably a good thing; too much sail area might stress the boat and rip it apart. "I'll take it," I said. Walking up front to pay, I passed a bin of moldering orange life jackets and thought of my first raft. "I'll take a couple of those, too," I told the salesman. "You never know."

ALL HANDS ON DECK

As the days dwindled down, more and more people came by to help. Garth and I started to delegate important jobs, including the training of new volunteers, to our most experienced people. With brief instructions and effusive thanks, we set them all on tasks that were hard and dirty. It didn't matter if someone was a Ph.D. or a chief of staff or a millionaire investor (and all of these showed up); they were all assigned menial work, usually on the floor. Many left with their hands raw and blistered, sometimes even bleeding.

And they loved it. There was an intensity to the Boat Works now, an infectious urgency that surprised people when they first showed up, but never failed to sweep them away. Having worked extensively with volunteers on campaigns, I knew that people want to feel needed and productive. We satisfied that desire by asking—almost demanding—a lot from them, perhaps more than was reasonable. It was a formula that usually brought out the best in people.

"Thank you for letting me be a part of this," said a guy I didn't know, the boyfriend of an acquaintance. He was in Washington only for the weekend and had just finished three hours of knot work on the garage floor, accidentally burning himself several times with one of the cheap lighters we used to melt the fraying ends of cut line. I deflected his thanks, expressing instead my gratitude for his help. But he was emphatic. He wouldn't accept my thanks. "No, thank *you*. It was just great. I only wish I could be here for the launch."

As launch day drew closer, Garth and I struggled to finalize a design. Working from our sketches, Garth put his AutoCAD skills to work, producing a series of detailed computer schematics that revealed an unexpected problem: we didn't have enough corks. Couldn't we just build a smaller boat? I asked. We had enough for buoyancy's sake. No, Garth insisted. We needed seventy thousand more corks to build four extra logs, for a total of nine. Only by interlocking nine logs in two layers, five on the bottom and four on top, could we achieve the honeycomb structure that would give the boat strength and stability.

It was a struggle for me to listen objectively. Garth may have been the most experienced designer, but I was the most experienced in cork sorting and assembly. I knew the manpower it would take to transform our existing corks into logs, let alone to sort and assemble another seventy thousand. At this point, we only had two logs completely finished, and time was running short. I had even started keeping track of the exact number of hours left before launch.

But if Garth said we needed nine logs, we probably did. Then, just to prove we could assemble them in time, he surprised me by working eighteen hours straight and disking more than eleven thousand corks on his own. Convinced now, I called up Chris at Cork Supply USA and, apologizing, explained our dilemma. Though I was reluctant to tell Chris that we couldn't use half the corks he had sent us already, there was no beating around the bush. We needed seventy thousand top-grade corks shipped via express delivery. And they would have to be presorted—there would be no time to pick out any agglomerates. I held my breath.

"You got it," Chris said, cheerfully. "I'll send them out tomorrow."

There were other pressing design and construction issues, too. In order to mount the mast and oarlocks, we had decided we needed a wooden deck over at least part of the boat. I told Garth that if he drew up plans, I'd hand them off to Harold, across the alley. "If we buy the lumber, he'll build it for us," I said.

Garth was doubtful. Why would that gruff neighbor, the one who was always complaining, be willing to spend eight or ten hours building a deck for the *Cork Boat*?

My thoughts flashed to all those hot summer days in the alley, and how a chance acquaintance had evolved into a warm friendship.

"Because I'll ask him, that's why," I said.

As the final week approached, Garth and I started pushing harder than ever—designing, delegating, recruiting, and building. I had all but abandoned my work on the Hill, though I had spent enough time there to require precautionary testing, along with my colleagues, for anthrax exposure. Following close on the heels of 9/11, an anthrax scare had shut one Senate office building entirely and left the entire city jittery, including me. So I was glad to spend the vast majority of my time at the Boat Works, miles away from the Capitol's domed bull's-eye. Garth was psyched to get out of his office, too, having cashed in the last of his precious vacation time for the home stretch.

Tired but motivated as we entered the final seven days, Garth and I fell into perfect sync, finally reveling in the intense camaraderie and challenge of our endeavor. As I had suspected when I first asked Garth to join the project, he proved to be a wild animal of a worker. Our earlier disputes melted away, and we gunned hard for the finish in tandem. Finally, we were both having fun. We even enjoyed sharing a near disaster, when an unevenly tensioned, twenty-foot log buckled into a spectacular S-curve. It held, though; and, together, like surgeons, we rescued it.

Pulling out all the stops, we also started spending money with abandon. Did we need 10,000 more feet of costly Dacron line FedExed from Boston? Well, what's another $500. Another case of number 64 rubber bands that Alliance declined to donate? Just put it on my Visa. Rope, oars, and more lumber for decking? Whatever they cost. We sent my friend Phil Guire out with a last-minute shopping list one day, and the bill came to more than $750. But we didn't care anymore.

Too soon, the Friday before Columbus Day arrived, and we were still way behind schedule. Our design didn't just call for nine simple logs; several of them featured great, sweeping curves that would ultimately form the boat's Viking-like prow.

Constructing these curves from thousands of uncooperative corks posed an extreme technical challenge. Although I had figured out how to build them, their execution was consuming more hours than we could afford. Contrary to our initial hopes, we had realized that we couldn't simply bend the logs. Although every log had a little flex, the curves Garth had designed were so dramatic that we had to build each one artisanally, interspersing specially designed "wedge disks," almost like the stone arches of medieval doorways.

Once assembled, we had to reinforce each angled joint with its own taut, net bandage, then rig the entire arch with a customized harness system that allowed us to compress it along its own, curving axis. Finally, we had to sew on a net sheath, just like the straight logs to which they would ultimately be grafted—an attachment process that we had not yet tested.

But even if we were running out of time, it was too late to scale back the design; if we were to scrap the curved prow, the boat would lose its dramatic Nordic profile, and both Garth and I had too much ego invested in the boat to settle for anything less than true nautical beauty. Our other option, postponing the launch a day or two, was also out of the question; we had already sent a team of volunteers out to distribute launch invitations at all the bars and restaurants that had donated corks. Like Garth's original SAVE YOUR CORKS flier, this was another understated masterpiece. Featuring the grainy scanned image of a cork we had found, one emblazoned with a simple stylized anchor, the flier read:

165,321 CORKS.

1 BOAT.

In smaller type, it gave the time and place of the launch, a public park in Annapolis. We had settled on Annapolis for three reasons. First, it offered us sheltered water on the Chesapeake. Second, the bay's saltwater would give our boat extra buoyancy. Third, we felt the Naval Academy's aura might add a certain something to our launch. Not that we had a boat to launch, yet. But we would. Maybe.

We worked straight through Friday night until just after five A.M. on Saturday, when we broke for a three-hour nap.

Four of nine logs were completely done. Two more were ready for netting. Three more logs remained to be built, though we had most of the hexagonal disks assembled and waiting. Most troubling, only a few had the curves we needed.

At nine A.M. we were back at work, with several volunteers at our side. I had put out a desperate yet confident "all hands on deck" summons to anybody and everybody who might volunteer.

This was the crunch, I'd told people. It's now or never. We need bodies, and lots of them. All day, and probably all night. And all day long, they kept showing up: friends, colleagues, spouses of colleagues, strangers, neighbors, family.

My dad flew in from a meeting in Arizona, and when he walked into the Boat Works for the first time and saw the scale of operations, a huge grin spread across his face.

"Not bad, H, is it?" I said, gesturing at the mayhem around us. (We often went by initials in my family.)

"Wow," was all he could say. "Wow!"

My mom flew in from Michigan, too. Earlier in the year, during a brief business trip to Washington, she had spent a long afternoon in the garage, assembling corks. She, too, was impressed by all the progress, and like my dad, ready for action. "Put me to work!" she said.

Similarly, Andy Nyblade—the friend who had invited me to Antarctica—drove down from State College, Pennsylvania, and a high school friend, Deb Nichols, flew in from Chicago. My cousin Tamar—Aunt Marlene's daughter—took the morning's first train down from New York and, relieved for the weekend getaway, settled into the grungiest corner of the garage, along with Jock, to finish grafting a curve onto one of the stern logs. Tamar, a singer and actor and self-described "fashionista," was not accustomed to hard physical labor, but she dug right in with gusto. Brandt, too, cleared his schedule and joined the fray.

The calls of support came in, too. My childhood friend Andrew, with whom I had built the SS *Milky Way,* phoned from Los Angeles to wish me luck. And Marlene, whose duties at her bed-and-breakfast, Schoenberger House, had kept her in Michigan, called in with her own final words of encouragement.

"This is so exciting, Johnny," she said. "I knew you could do it! I *knew* you could do it!"

Even amidst my exhaustion, I was keenly aware that we were creating something special. Not just a boat, but a day—a team—that we would all remember. As my mom pointed out, marveling at all the activity spilling out of the garage and into the alley, I had gathered all of America in one place, at least symbolically. There were men and women; little kids and retirees; Democrats and Republicans; people who were gay, straight, black, white, Asian, and Hispanic; wealthy and working class; Jewish, Muslim, and Christian. There was even a Hungarian there, for good measure.

"It's more than diversity," my mom said. "People in Washington sort themselves into camps. Most of them don't speak to each other, and when they do, they usually don't have anything nice to say. But they're here in this alley now, pulling and tugging and tying knots together, all for one idea."

The truth is, I *was* proud to have motivated all these people, to have brought them together for a project that was at once so preposterous and so sublime. But I didn't really have time to savor the moment—the sun would be down soon, and we would start losing volunteers. We couldn't afford that; the last logs weren't even assembled, and the clock was ticking.

At six P.M., Garth and I walked around the block for a powwow. We always walked around the block when we needed a break. Walking helped us clear our heads, and in this case it gave us a chance to talk through our situation in privacy, out of earshot from our volunteers. Strung out from lack of sleep, I was pretty distraught.

Deep in discussion, we ran into Zoë, who had shown up to lend a hand. "How's it going?" she asked, doubtful and sweet and supportive all at once.

"I don't think we're going to make it," I said.

"We can make it," Garth answered.

"You think so?" I asked.

"Yes. But it's going to get ugly."

His grim optimism, kicking in just as mine ran empty, tipped the balance. This was the never-say-die Garth that I loved. No matter how much we had fought, I had always known he'd be good in the clutch.

At this point, we really didn't have any choice but to keep pushing. TV stations had been calling my cell phone all day, wanting launch details. The fliers were out. People had traveled a long way for the launch—not just friends and family, but even Chris Sipola, from Cork Supply USA.

Just as important, we had thirty people around the corner working flat out because we told them this boat absolutely had to launch tomorrow, no matter what. We couldn't just give up now and pull the plug. There was no way through but through.

Our original game plan was shot; it was time for the no-huddle offense. We would have to start calling audibles at the line. Our last deadline, the only one that mattered now, was tomorrow morning, nine A.M. That's when the boat mover we'd hired for $900 was scheduled to roll up the alley with a trailer to carry the boat to Annapolis for the afternoon launch.

Our biggest remaining obstacle was weight. Some of our longest logs (still under construction) would probably weigh over 300 pounds and would be extremely awkward to lift and position. When they were lashed together in threes, what we called "trinities," we'd be dealing with twenty-two-foot components weighing over 700 pounds apiece.

That meant, at minimum, we would need ten volunteers to stay through the night, just to lift the logs into place for final assembly. We made a mental list of those we thought would stick it out. A lot of people were already exhausted. Some, like Garth and me, had been up for almost thirty-six hours straight. Others were suffering a range of maladies: their backs were aching, their heads were pounding, their hands were swollen or burned. To make matters worse, a cold front was blowing in and the temperature was dropping fast. Stay through the bitter end? Our list came to seven or eight.

Topping the list were Garth's two climbing buddies, Curtis Runyan and Keegan Eisenstadt. They both had strength and swagger and would stick it out, no matter what. On top of that, they knew how to tie knots. And they were relatively fresh—they'd arrived just a few hours earlier.

We rounded the corner, back into the alley, as the sun began to set.

"Listen up, team," I announced, running now on coffee and adrenaline. "We're doing great. We're making good progress. It's going to be tight, but we're going to make it. We have pizza on its way, and extra clothes if you get cold. Garth and I are really, really grateful for all your help. Just keep going."

And in the last, fading light of day, Garth, Curtis, Keegan, my dad, and I crowded around the old table we'd dragged into the alley as a field headquarters, since the garage had become too crowded with construction. Laying out three hexagonal cork disks to represent the cross sections of three adjacent logs, I took a piece of cord and demonstrated the complex, looping pattern that, theoretically, would lash the logs together. Garth and I called this pattern a "trinity lashing." Keegan—king of knots—got it right away and even suggested a way to make it simpler. Facing the prospect of cutting, positioning, and tying a total of three hundred lashings, we were all for simplification. "Great call," I said. "Go for it."

Leaving Curtis and Keegan in charge of the trinity lashings, Garth and I mustered another ten people to help wrestle the first three complete logs into place. The trinities required careful alignment, as each log's dimensions and curves played a specific role in the overall structure of the boat. Ultimately, the boat would be composed of three trinities, belted together like a three-dimensional jigsaw puzzle. According to Garth's final schematics, the whole boat would fit together like a honeycomb.

Our immediate challenge was that every lashing—and there were a hundred lashings per trinity—had to be set in place and tightened simultaneously. That meant leaving a few inches of space between three heavy logs, holding them just above the floor until the last possible moment, when the lashings were to be tightened. It was a seven-hundred-pound, technical and organizational nightmare, one we would have to repeat to assemble each of our three trinities.

Garth said he had an idea, but we would need bricks. Lots of bricks. We would use them as spacers between logs. Now, hauling several hundred pounds of brick is unpleasant work under the best of circumstances; but hauling them out of his crammed, junk-filled co-op basement was truly miserable. Together, we got the job done. But it took its toll on our volunteer corps. One by one, people started begging off for the night.

By now it was totally dark, and even though the garage had lights, a shortage of space had led us to requisition a neighbor's garage, too. Unfortunately, that garage—and our work area in the alley itself—lacked electricity, so people had to sew the last logs shut by candlelight. But nobody complained. Everybody was too focused on his or her own specific task. Across the alley, I could hear the whine of Harold's circular saw biting into sheets of plywood. He was building our deck.

Shortly after ten the little neighbor boys, Walter and Ezra, came walking up the alley with their mother. Earlier in the day, we had enlisted them to pass out launch fliers to all the neighbors on the block. Now it was way past their bedtime, but this was a big night. They carried Styrofoam cups for all of us, which their mom filled with cappuccino from a thermos.

Everybody gave them a round of applause. Their innocent good cheer, and the jolt of caffeine, got us going again. And then it struck me: I had been Ezra's age when I first imagined this boat made of wine corks. How quickly life goes, I thought. How quickly the night, too. In the next half-hour we lost a few more people.

By eleven, it was clear that Garth's idea to use bricks as spacers between the logs took considerable time to set up, but might actually work. At midnight a bunch of us pulled one hundred trinity lashings tight, knotted them in place, and let out a cheer. The first trinity was done.

My parents, who had been cutting trinity lashings for

several hours, called it a night. I walked them to the end of the alley, and thanked them for everything. And I meant everything—the years of saving corks, their faith in me and the boat project, and for making the trip.

"We'll see you in the morning," my dad said. "We're so proud of you." That meant a lot, coming from him. I could remember when he thought the boat was, if not a waste of time, at least keeping me from pursuing a "real job." I told them I hoped I hadn't summoned them to Washington for nothing.

Returning to the Boat Works, I took a head count. We were down to eleven people, all working with determination. Three long, hard hours later, the second trinity was done, but there were only nine of us left. There was no cheer this time, only a short break while I sewed the netting of the last log shut. Meanwhile, Curtis's girlfriend had reached her limit and he announced they would have to go. That was a big blow, but we understood. Listening to his car disappear around the corner into the night, I tried my best to ignore the desperation of our situation.

Severely shorthanded now, we struggled just to move the final logs into place for lashing. Composed of four logs, despite its name, this was the heaviest, most awkward trinity of them all—the boat's middle section, featuring a sweeping, seven-foot prow and a bifurcated keel log that would permit us to insert a centerboard. Every muscle ached. Every joint throbbed. And everyone was getting slaphappy, some reduced to eating the last, gnawed crusts of cold pizza. I looked at my watch, almost delirious. It was going on four. At least we'd get some light in a few hours.

When a new DJ came on the radio and put on Ricky Martin, a howl of protest erupted, as if we'd all been doused with a bucket of ice water. Suddenly, the absurdity of the situation, the desperation with which we were working, the sheer determination to build the *Cork Boat,* seemed utterly hilarious. We started laughing. At ourselves. At the project. At life. We would get this damned boat done. We just weren't sure exactly how, or when.

Just then a pair of headlights flashed around the corner, down the alley, and a familiar, rusting Subaru emerged from the gloom. "Curtissssss!" we yelled.

"I couldn't leave you guys," he said, climbing out, grinning. He had dropped his exhausted girlfriend off at her apartment and had come back to help us finish the job. Even with Curtis, though, it was a back-breaking slog. But just before six, the final trinity was done.

Now all that was left was the moment of truth: final assembly. Would the three trinities fit together? Could we even lift them into position?

Together, all eight of us—six men and two women—struggled to move the last, massive trinity. At first it seemed impossible, but slowly, step by step, grunting and cursing, we maneuvered that twenty-two-foot behemoth out of the garage and into position, between the others. I was extraordinarily grateful when it fit with the other two, just like a puzzle. For the first time, it actually looked something like a boat.

From that point it took us only an hour to lash them together into a single unit with cargo belts, the kind with a geared, buckle-like ratchet device called a "come-along" that lets truckers cinch their loads down tight. Then four of us placed Harold's deck on top and belted that down, too.

Finally, as Garth and I set the mast in place, I looked up the alley to see the deep-blue sky of dawn creeping, just barely, over the rooftops. Keegan started chanting, and—sleeping neighbors be damned—we all joined in, crazy with jubilation: *"Cork Boat! Cork Boat! Cork Boat!"*

My watch said seven A.M. We had made it! The world's first cork boat was done.

And it was beautiful. Beautiful and big. Bigger than I had ever imagined. Bigger even than the neighbor's swimming pool in which I had envisioned launching it thirty years earlier. All but sleepless for the past forty-eight hours now, I struggled to grasp what I was seeing. This was the real thing, my *Cork Boat*. All I could do was gape.

But when we stood back to admire our creation from a short distance, we noticed a slight problem. In our exhaustion, we had misaligned one of the curving bow logs. Viewed from the front, the boat's prow appeared slightly asymmetrical. In fact, it looked strikingly like the knuckles and finger of an enormous hand, flipping us the bird.

"Oops," Garth said.

We laughed. There was nothing we could do about it, at least not now.

With two hours until the boat mover was due, I drove home to take a shower and an hour's nap. When I got back up to the Boat Works at eight-thirty, my parents were already there, snapping pictures. Having arrived at eight, uncertain whether the boat would even be done, they were ecstatic.

But they *had* noticed the boat giving them the finger. "Rounding the corner," my dad said, "I saw the boat giving the finger, and I thought to myself: Fuck you, Osama bin Laden."

In daylight, the Boat Works looked like a disaster zone, strewn with loose corks, scraps of netting, tangled line, torn pizza boxes, scattered bricks, dirty coffee mugs, various tools, and the odd rubber glove. Sorting through this mess, we gathered the tools necessary to rig the boat, plus anything else we thought we might possibly need for the launch in Annapolis.

How we had done it, I couldn't quite say. Two days earlier, only two logs were done. Now, thanks to so many people, we had a twenty-two-foot boat.

AFLOAT

S ometime after ten A.M., the boat mover finally showed
up with his truck and trailer. As he stepped out of his
vehicle for the first time, I was taken aback. He was a giant.
He must have stood six-foot-six and weighed over three hundred pounds, and he had an attitude to match his paunch. He
took one look at the boat, Garth and I took one look at his
trailer, and we all knew that ours was a match made in hell.

"I've moved America's Cup yachts. I've moved submarines.
But I've never seen anything like this boat. I can't move it," the
giant declared.

He was right. Despite my description and instructions over
the phone, he had brought a traditional, cradle-shaped boat
trailer that—over the potholes of local freeways—would probably rip our flat-bottomed boat apart long before it ever
arrived in Annapolis. It didn't help that the boat itself turned
out to be two feet longer than we had planned.

As Garth and I held a hushed meeting, the giant waited
impatiently down the alley, whacking at his trailer with a

crowbar, trying to loosen up some rusty bolts. "If we're going to do this, we've got a lot of work to modify this trailer," he called out. "Is there a Home Depot nearby?" He was probably thinking of the $900 he stood to lose. This was an agonizing choice. I couldn't stand not to launch, not after what we had gone through to finish the boat. But the thought of ruining it before it even hit the water was worse yet. And it was too late to look for another hauler. We'd have to cancel the launch. For a hundred-dollar kill fee, the giant drove off, his empty trailer clattering behind.

Garth and I stood there, a little dumbfounded. This was too much. We knew we had to come up with a new plan, and fast. People were expecting a launch. In fact, dozens of our volunteers were probably leaving within the hour to meet us over in Annapolis. Meanwhile, here we were, our boat stuck high and dry in a shabby alley, forty-five miles from the Chesapeake. I felt like Robinson Crusoe, stranded on that island: his first boat, which had taken him months to build, was so big he couldn't drag it to the water. Hell, we couldn't even drag our boat back into the garage—it probably weighed more than two thousand pounds.

"What about a dry launch?" my mom offered—a launch party right here in the alley, complete with champagne. "People have put in too much not to have a party," she said. "The boat is done. Let's celebrate."

She was right. It was the best we could do. In fact, it was an inspired idea. We got on our various phones to head people off. My dad and I drove out to the launch site, in Annapolis, to catch those we missed. When we pulled back into the alley a few hours later, there was the mighty *Cork Boat,* surrounded by sixty or seventy people, drinks in hand, having a great time.

The garage was spotless, with our schematics proudly on display, pinned to a corkboard. Apparently, my mom had taken charge of a volunteer crew to clean things up. Somewhere in the mess, she had come across a small boat made of bundled reeds, a toy I had brought home decades earlier from one of our trips to Peru. I had retrieved it from Ann Arbor some months earlier, thinking perhaps that it might hold design clues for the *Cork Boat.* Thoughtfully, my mom had put it on display.

There were also platters of food and coolers full of beer, wine, and champagne. Andrea Felix, one of Garth's housemates and a member of the "enduring eight" who had stuck it out all night, sewing by candlelight, had mustered the energy to bake a celebratory sheet cake. Its frosting resembled our flier's anchor motif and included our new motto: "165,321 corks. 1 boat."

Using a wooden dowel as a pole (a dowel originally intended as a ramrod for packing corks into the failed tubular loading system), I hung an American flag off the garage. It was the same flag that I had hung in my mom's campaign headquarters when she was running for the U.S. Senate, years earlier. That campaign, too, had been a spirited team effort of dedicated volunteers, one whose final hours had stretched until dawn. It, too, had come up just short.

I opened a bottle of beer, and for the first time in six weeks, truly relaxed. Chris Sipola, from Cork Supply USA, showed up, flabbergasted at our creation. He shot two rolls of film and just kept muttering: "It's amazing! It's amazing."

Garth and I eventually climbed atop the boat, grateful and giddy, to thank the assembled crowd and Cork Supply USA for making it all possible. We popped a magnum of champagne, a gift from one of our volunteers, and doused the boat. Just then, the two men we had been missing came striding around the corner. It was Curtis and Keegan, and the crowd cheered.

Again, we broke into a victory chant: *"Cork Boat! Cork Boat! Cork Boat!"*

It was a moment to savor, and a party to remember. I was only a little regretful about the dry launch; we had built the *Cork Boat,* and it was more magnificent than I could ever have imagined. Exhausted, I lay down on the boat and watched the fall leaves drifting down, lazily, from the blue sky. And then I was asleep.

I woke up the next day in my own bed, my hands still blistered and swollen, my knees aching, my back sore. But I felt an enormous sense of relief. Checking my voice mail, I found a message from Zoë. Always generous of spirit, she had called to offer her congratulations: ". . . It's a beautiful boat, and I hope you're proud. It makes me realize that all the times I said maybe don't strive so hard, that you didn't need to scale back, that you could pull it off. So I hope you're feeling good about it, and that you let the accomplishment sink in."

And I did, for the first few days. But a week later, the *Cork Boat* was still in the alley. The neighbors hadn't complained—not yet, anyway. But the garbagemen could barely get their truck through, and after another photo appeared in the *Washington Post* we started worrying about vandalism.

Garth and I went back and forth on what to do. We couldn't just leave the boat where it was. But moving it wouldn't be easy, either. And with my departure for Antarctica fast approaching, we had to make a decision.

"Let's get this boat in the water," I argued. "A boat's not a boat unless it's in the water."

Garth, busy catching up at work, wasn't in as much of a hurry. But since we had to move it anyway, he conceded that we might as well put it in the water before putting it in storage. But no hoopla this time, he insisted. While we had thrown a pretty good party, our "dry launch" hadn't quite lived up to all the original hype. I agreed. We would organize a quiet, Sunday-afternoon sea trial, this time down on the Potomac.

Forced to improvise a new way to transport the boat, we made a Thursday-night run out to Home Depot—or, as Garth enjoyed calling it, Home Despot. Although we were pressed for time and the long drive out to the suburbs was hell, even at night, I really loved that store. Not because the staff there knew anything—it was practically impossible to get assistance, let alone good advice. No, I loved Home Despot because its abundance spoke to my sense of possibility. Looking around at acres of tools and building materials, I figured we could build Noah's Ark if we had to. We settled for ten of the heaviest furniture dollies they sold, and a bag of nuts and bolts to double them up.

Somehow, we were going to lift that boat—all two thousand pounds of it—off the ground and slip the dollies underneath. Whether it was because people were all cork-boated out or that we were recruiting at the last minute for a Saturday night, Garth and I could only turn out a single volunteer, the ever dependable Jock Friedly. Together, the three of us worked through the night, using six manual car jacks simultaneously to lift the boat up, section by section. In the process, we crushed two jacks—and almost one Jock—when the boat, unstable on the alley's sloping pavement, shifted and fell. Who knew that cork was stronger than steel?

Without a full crew, it was a hellacious night. But when the trucker we had hired showed up on Sunday morning, our boat had five dollies strapped beneath it, totaling forty wheels. This time, instead of hiring a boat mover, I had called Abe's Towing—a towing company whose largest truck was a "rollback" carrier boasting a heavy-duty electric winch and a hydraulic flatbed that tilted back like a ramp. It was our only, best, and last shot at transportation.

Loading went relatively smoothly, and was over in half an hour. Once we had lashed the boat down securely, to keep it from rolling off mid-journey, I climbed into the cab with the driver, Salah, for the short trip to Virginia. We were going to launch in the Potomac at Belle Haven Marina, just south of Old Town Alexandria. Fittingly, Salah turned out to be an Egyptian immigrant who had grown up along the Nile. He had a love for boats, and our bizarre craft was no exception.

As we drove, we talked about Egypt. It was one of the most interesting places I had ever visited. I told him that archaeologists had recently discovered the world's oldest ship there, buried in the desert. It was more than five thousand years old. In fact, I had read, the Egyptians were probably the first people to develop a boat with oars, rudder, mast, and sail. Even earlier, they had built boats from bundled reeds along the Nile. Salah took it all in with the modesty of a man who knows he comes from a culture as old as human memory.

Suddenly, our conversation was interrupted. Just ahead, by the side of the road, was a police car, lights flashing. The officer was flagging us down.

I knew right away what was going on. It was only six weeks after 9/11, and the police were still jittery. Our load—this strange, giant object—must have looked suspicious rolling down the George Washington Parkway. Salah's ethnicity wouldn't necessarily inspire confidence, either.

Salah pulled over, the truck's tires crunching to a stop on the gravel shoulder. I climbed down from the cab, and approached the officer. "It's the world's first cork boat," I explained, preemptively. "I'm taking it to Belle Haven Marina for its maiden launch."

Gruff and suspicious, she looked me over. I was wearing shorts and an American-flag T-shirt. I didn't look like a terrorist, but . . .

"Do you have a permit?" she snapped.

"A permit?" I asked. I didn't know I needed a permit.

"Who did you talk to?" she countered, testily.

Talk to? What was she talking about? I'd have to play dumb and confident, at once.

"I talked to Belle Haven Marina," I said. "They said I could launch . . . Look, it's just a boat made out of 165,000 wine corks and a lot of rubber bands."

Her face was stone. I was getting nowhere. Suddenly, she broke into a grin and started laughing.

"Get out of here!" she said, waving us on. "Just don't come back this way!"

Half an hour later, as a dozen friends and a handful of bystanders watched, Salah slowly unwound the truck's electric winch. Little by little, the boat rolled backward off the tilted flatbed, and into the water.

Standing thigh deep in water on the submerged ramp, I

helped guide the boat as it slid off the truck. I wanted to make sure the wheels on the dollies didn't catch. Suddenly, it was floating free, a boat in the water. I was aboard in an instant, and Garth too, our arms raised in triumph.

"*Cork Boat!*" we yelled.

Somebody handed us a bottle of champagne. Rather than swing the bottle against the resilient cork prow, we sent its cork shooting into the sky, doused the bow thoroughly with the spouting bubbly, and passed the bottle around. For once, I was at a loss for words.

This was sheer glory. Pure elation. Whatever might happen next, I decided, it didn't matter. I had seen this one through, start to finish. The *Cork Boat* was in the water. And it floated like—what else?—a cork.

I called my parents on my cell phone, to share the moment. Talking a mile a minute, I told them I had never imagined that building the boat would be so agonizingly difficult, so full of conflict, or generate so much camaraderie. It was an incredibly satisfying moment. Not just for me, but for so many others, even the strangers who stood watching, dumbstruck, this odd craft before them.

As we tied the boat up along the dock, a man approached me to offer congratulations. "I've been saving corks for years," he said, excitedly. "And my roommate always gives me grief. He's always made fun of me, asking, 'What are you saving all those corks for?' Now I can tell him—I'm saving them to build a *Cork Boat!*"

We spent the next couple of hours taking people for rides, testing the oars and sail, and reveling in the glory of the day. And it was a glorious day, even if the oars were too small, the sail ineffectual, and our teaspoon of a rudder unable to bring the boat about. The *Cork Boat* floated, and that's what mattered, even if we did require a tow back to shore.

Finally, the afternoon growing short, we phoned Salah, and waited for the truck to return. Loading the boat back onto the truck was surprisingly easy, and the trip back to the Boat Works was uneventful. In fact, Salah was able to unload the boat right into the garage. It didn't quite fit inside—the prow stuck out into the alley—but no matter. We'd figure out a way to shut the door later, or build a new one, before winter. But that was a challenge for tomorrow.

The next week flashed past quickly, as I wrapped up my work for Congressman Bonior and packed my gear for Antarctica. Bonior, at a small going-away party on Friday, congratulated me on the boat and thanked me for coming back to rejoin the office when he needed me.

I thanked him warmly; not only had he given me a job when I really needed one, he had also given me the chance to serve at a time when the country needed everyone to pitch in, in whatever way they could. Working through 9/11 had been a profoundly moving experience. I confessed, though, that "I still don't know what I'm going to do when I grow up."

"Sure you do," Bonior said. "You're doing it. And doing it well. You're building cork boats and going to Antarctica."

Late the next morning, I drove over to the Boat Works to help Garth close up shop. When I pulled into the alley, he was already staple-gunning wire fencing over the open door of the garage; we covered the fencing with a tarp, and stapled that in place, too. I told Garth that our boat was like the billionaire Howard Hughes's experimental *Spruce Goose*, the 700-passenger wooden seaplane whose wingspan stretched the length of an entire football field, and then some. It flew only once—on a 1947 test run over Long Beach Harbor—but proved all of its doubters wrong. They had predicted it would never fly. We had proven our doubters wrong, too, and could be just as proud.

Still, as leaves swirled against a gray sky, there was a melancholy feel to the moment. As we said goodbye—emotionally and physically drained—neither of us could know that the journey of the *Cork Boat* was only just beginning. That boat wasn't done with us yet. Not by a long shot.

ANTARCTICA

A little more than a week after leaving Washington, I found myself stepping out of an Air National Guard transport onto the frozen sea ice of McMurdo Sound, just off the coast of Antarctica's Ross Island.

If my immediate surroundings over the past few months had been defined by the close, grimy walls of the Boat Works, the boundless, windswept horizons of Antarctica presented a radically different reality. Leaving a bustling city beset by anthrax and anxiety, I had arrived to a continental frozen wasteland where the only white powder was the whipping snow that stung my face like tiny shards of glass.

The scientific team I had joined was aiming to install a network of solar-powered seismometers in the continent's interior. The goal was to map the structure of the earth beneath the Trans-Antarctic Mountains, a jagged range cutting halfway across the continent. The Trans-Antarctics form the only mountain range in the world not caused by the collision of tectonic plates, the shifting puzzle-like pieces that make up the earth's crust. With data from these seismometers, scientists were hoping to answer, within the next few years, one central question: Why are the Trans-Antarctic Mountains rising?

Our job was to set up the instruments and their solar panels at regular intervals along a five-hundred-mile route, securing them against winds that could top a hundred miles per hour. And although the era of dogsleds had long since passed and we traveled by ski-plane and helicopter, our work on the ground was still cold, hard, and unforgiving.

I knew well the chilling stories of the early polar explorers. My favorite was that of Sir Ernest Shackleton, whose ship *Endurance* had been crushed by ice and sank before he even reached the Antarctic continent. His epic five-month voyage of survival in 1914–15, first on ice floes and then in a small open boat through the stormiest seas on earth, was the stuff of legend.

I had also read the bitter saga of Captain Robert Falcon Scott, who, in 1912, in a brutal race to be the first to reach the South Pole, arrived a month too late, beaten by his Norwegian rival Roald Amundsen. Scott and his companions ran out of food on the way home and froze to death, just eleven miles from a supply depot.

Discovered alongside Scott's frozen corpse the following spring was a note that read, in part:

For my own sake I do not regret this journey, which has shown that Englishmen can endure hardships, help one another, and meet death with as great a fortitude as ever in the past. We took risks, we knew we took them; things have come out against us, and therefore we have no cause for complaint, but bow to the will of providence, determined still to do our best to the last. . . . Had we lived, I should have had a tale to tell of the hardihood, endurance, and courage of my companions which would have stirred the heart of every Englishman. These rough notes and our dead bodies must tell the tale. . . .

Surprisingly, the wooden hut from which Scott and his companions had set off on their ill-fated trek was still standing on a windswept cape located on Cape Evans, just a few miles from McMurdo Station, the American scientific base from which we operated. On a rare afternoon off, I hitched a ride over there on a giant snow machine and slipped inside for a look.

Although some ninety winters had passed since Scott had last crossed its threshold, the cold had preserved everything. Fur sleeping bags lay atop snug dry bunks, and a pair of wool socks hung, forever drying, from a rusty nail. A yellowed, paperback copy of *Jane Eyre* lay open and facedown beneath a bed, as if waiting for its long-dead reader to return. On shelves near a cast-iron stove, boxes of macaroni, cans of corned beef, and tins of cocoa testified to the hearty appetites of the dead adventurers. And on another shelf I spotted a very familiar-looking bottle of Heinz ketchup standing sentry over jars of a strange condiment called "India Relish."

Something about the ketchup bottle caught my eye. Although the 1911 label was almost identical to those in a modern supermarket, the bottle was . . . I leaned in for a closer look . . . *yes*, sealed with a cork! It was the only thing that made me smile in that somber hut.

If modern technology had made Antarctic work easier and safer in the intervening years, experienced hands still took the environment very, very seriously. Safety was not something left to chance. Wherever we got dropped off, often in bleak surroundings as flat and white as bone china, we always made sure to unload a pair of red "survival bags"—heavy vinyl duffels containing mountain tents, stoves, food, sleeping bags, and an extra radio. In typical working conditions, about thirty-five degrees below zero (Fahrenheit) in calm air, they weren't necessary. But should the weather turn bad and prevent the aircraft from making a timely return, that gear could keep us alive for days.

Not that "good" weather in the Antarctic summer was very pleasant. Scott had written, "Great God, this is an awful place!" and his description proved true. Although the sun never set during summer, it was still so cold that my goggles often iced over in minutes, exposed skin became painful within seconds, and heavy, insulated boots did little to keep my feet from turning to leaden blocks of throbbing misery.

Despite such discomforts and the potential dangers of polar travel, I loved the beauty and adventure of it all, especially flying over the rugged landscape by helicopter. The mountains were endless and jagged, and the glaciers—some thirty miles wide—meandered like mighty frozen rivers until they disappeared over horizons a hundred miles distant.

Thumping through the sky, I always knew the comforts of civilization were close at hand when I could spot Mount Erebus, the towering volcanic peak that looms above McMurdo. From the air, the base looked something like a small, hardscrabble mining town, a gritty place of utilitarian buildings, monster trucks, heavy equipment, fuel tanks, and shipping containers. On the ground, it reminded me of an international truck stop at the end of the world, a bizarre crossroads of physicists, welders, biologists, cooks, mountain guides, volunteer firemen, geologists, hermits, and some hard-drinking crews from the Air National Guard.

Every time I landed in McMurdo after a hard, cold day in the field, I felt I had earned the right to what few bourgeois pleasures were to be found there. Apart from a warm meal and a hot shower (with a two-minute limit!), my favorite indulgence was the former officers' club—a cozy, corrugated Quonset hut decorated with wooden skis, weathered ice-axes, and vintage sleds from the 1950s. With dim lighting and a little jazz on the boom box, it easily achieved the best atmosphere on the continent. I also liked the place because it served both cappuccino and wine. The coffee warmed me up. The wine, of course, meant corks.

Technically speaking, the boat was done. Finished. Complete. But old habits die hard, and I just couldn't resist pocketing a few. If I added them to the boat, I reasoned, it would contain corks from every one of the world's seven continents.

Then again, maybe I had been on the ice too long.

Weighing Anchor

After almost two months in Antarctica, I returned to the United States. The excitement of getting home, though, gave way quickly to grim news: my Aunt Marlene was due for major heart surgery. Although the operation went relatively well for a woman of sixty-three, tests revealed that she also had a growing brain tumor. The doctors had discovered it too late, and there was nothing they could do.

Weakened by heart surgery, struggling against the metastasizing tumor, and suddenly confronting the certainty of her own death, Marlene's buoyant optimism and spirit of play abandoned her. It was a depressing, bitter end for someone who had lived life with such a perpetual twinkle in her eye. She spent her last few weeks in an Ann Arbor hospice as her daughter, Tamar, my parents, and I took turns sitting by her bedside.

We were all in the room when, gasping terrible, last breaths, she died. A friend of hers named Peter "Madcat" Ruth, a gifted blues harmonica player, happened to be there when the moment came. So as we all sobbed, Marlene passed away to the soft blue strains of "Amazing Grace."

I was among those who spoke at her funeral. I recalled her "spark for life, her subtle mirth, and her catchy enthusiasm." I told of the time, a few years earlier, when she traveled to New York to perform in Tamar's cabaret act. Marlene played the congas, which she had studied in Harlem, back in her college days. In our family, this particular show was a big deal. We'd all seen Tamar perform, but there hadn't been a Schoenberger duo onstage in nearly forty years, not since Marlene and my mom were in high school. So my mom flew in from Michigan, my dad stopped off on his way back from Russia, and I took the train up from Washington.

"Well, the big night came," I said, starting to cry. "And there, in a little club in the West Village, we applauded Tamar and cheered on Marlene as she beat those drums with all the joy of a lifetime. Watching Marlene play was the very picture of life at its finest—our family together, happy and proud; the rhythm of life beating strong within all of us. And I knew then that that evening was all the sweeter, because it was just that, one evening—a fleeting moment—in a life racing by. Now Marlene's drums are silent. But her spirit still beats in my heart."

Weeks after the service, sorting through her house, we found a small bag of corks, tucked away in a drawer. Marlene had saved them for my boat.

———

About a month later, some speechwriting work took me out to Palo Alto, California, for a few weeks. Since Cork Supply USA was located in Benicia, just fifty miles north, I decided to pay a visit. I wanted to meet my benefactors, see their operation, and thank them for all their support. I had another motive, too. In a recent e-mail, Chris had asked if Garth and I were still thinking about an overseas journey. I said that we hoped to organize one, but couldn't really afford to without sponsorship. He hadn't responded directly, but did mention he'd been talking up the boat with the company owner. It sounded like a hint.

Coincidentally, Garth was in Berkeley at the same time, checking out Cal's graduate program in architecture, so I called Chris and set up lunch for the three of us. At the last minute, Garth bailed—his schedule was just too tight to work in a trip to Benicia—so I drove up alone. Fighting midday traffic up 680, I crossed the Sacramento River toward Benicia, which, a brown sign informed me, had been California's first capital.

Off to my right, a mile or so up the river, were twenty-five or thirty ships, apparently derelict, anchored in a cluster midstream. Some were merchant freighters, others military gray. Had they been mothballed for salvage, or for use in times of conflict?

Honking cars brought me back to the moment. After paying the toll at the end of the bridge, I followed my directions
to a nondescript industrial park along the water, Cork Supply
USA's home base. I hadn't known what to expect, but definitely something more romantic than a series of modern
warehouses and the rumbling trucks that came and went. Yet
the view was not without a touch of the bizarre: there, standing knee-deep in the marsh, just beyond the railroad tracks,
was a huge, life-size Brontosaurus.

Chris gave me the full tour. The number of corks in the
Cork Supply warehouse staggered me. There were, literally,
tens of millions of them in the big burlap sacks I knew so well,
stacked on row after row of metal shelves that rose to a ceiling
fifty feet overhead. "This is awesome," I said. And I meant
awesome in the true sense of the word—it inspired awe. For
someone who worked in the cork industry, it was no big deal.
For a guy who had saved corks one by one most of his life, it
was almost beyond comprehension.

"There's a boat right there," Chris joked, pointing to a pallet taller than I was.

"Hell, there's a whole cork navy here," I answered.

On our way back across the parking lot to the Cork Supply
factory, I asked Chris about the giant dinosaur out in the
swamp. It was fiberglass, he said. It had originally stood watch
over a gas station in the Central Valley, until bulldozers razed
the place for a new subdivision. A group of pop-culture pre-
servationists had organized a rescue to save the extinct vege-

tarian, enlisting a giant chopper from the Air National Guard to airlift it to its new home.

Inside the noisy Cork Supply factory, automatic ink machines ker-chunked away at top speed, grabbing corks with pincers and imprinting them with the names of wines and wineries. Electric forklifts whirred about, shifting heavy pallets of cork. There were cork washing machines, giant tumble driers, and conveyor belts that rattled along with thousands and thousands of corks every minute. A dozen seated women watched, eagle-eyed, as the corks raced past, snatching away those that didn't meet quality standards. Having spent many long hours sorting corks myself, I really felt for them—and envied their technology. It sure beat the secondhand table we had used back in the Boat Works.

I liked seeing all those reject corks; they were the type that Cork Supply had given us for the boat. I watched a few good ones bounce off the assembly line. Upon hitting the floor they, too, became rejects, Chris said. More corks for the boat, I thought. I felt a real attachment to—even affection for—these inanimate objects, as if each one were an ally or coconspirator in my schemes.

"What happens to all the rejects that don't end up in cork boats?" I asked.

"We sell them to a dealer in Mexico," Chris said. "He has workers who sand off the printing, and he resells them. Obviously, labor is a little cheaper there."

On a congressional fact-finding mission a few years back, I

had visited the *maquiladoras* in Juarez, where workers earned five dollars a day in "good" jobs for American multinationals. Many of them lived in cardboard boxes salvaged from the factories where they worked. I didn't want to think about how little the cork sanders might be paid.

After lunch, talk turned to the boat, and Chris came straight out with an offer. He had spoken with Jochen Michalski, the owner. Cork Supply was interested in sponsoring a cork boat trip across Portugal—down the Douro River, specifically. Michalski would pay to ship the boat over, and Cork Supply's staff in Portugal would help us with all the local logistics.

"How does that sound?" Chris asked, grinning. "Are you interested?"

"Absolutely!" I said, thanking him profusely before unleashing a blizzard of questions. I didn't know much about the Douro River, except that—in Spain, at least—it boasted some of the finest castles on the entire Iberian peninsula. A decade earlier, when I had been working in Spain as a foreign correspondent, I hitchhiked up to a village on the river called Berlanga del Duero, and loved it.

There was only one catch: Cork Supply was planning a client trip to Portugal in June, and they wanted the boat there in time to show it off. June was only six weeks away, but June it would be. There were a thousand details to work through, from preparing the boat to researching the river to figuring out how to get the boat over there and into position. For the moment, though, the only thing that mattered was that the *Cork Boat* was going to Portugal. We would put things in motion immediately.

As soon as I pulled out of the industrial park, I laid on the car horn in glee, long blasts that probably scared the hell out of other drivers. I called Garth on his cell phone but got his voice mail. My message was short and jubilant: "Brother, we have sponsorship! Cork Supply wants to send the boat to Portugal. Call me!"

Calling my parents and everybody else I could think of to share the good news, I couldn't quite believe I was actually pulling this caper off. I thought of how Sara and I had started saving corks, one by one, in that wooden bowl in the kitchen. And then how, as an adult, I had actually quit my job to make the boat reality. All those days of drudgery and doubt, in the sleet and the scorching sun, collecting corks and feigning optimism even as I felt like quitting—all of it had paid off.

It was incredibly satisfying to think back to all those times I told people I was building the world's first cork boat and was going to sail it through European wine country. So many had dismissed that as idle boasting, or at best a pipe dream. Now it was coming true. I thought, too, of Marlene and how thrilled she'd be. She had always believed that I would pull it off.

It was nearing the end of April, and there was a lot to get done between then and Portugal. I had to get ahold of Garth. I left another message. One day passed, and then two. No call from Garth. I called Brandt, who told me Garth was still on the road, visiting grad schools, and having a terrible time making up his mind. "Tell him to call me!" I said. What was up?

When Garth finally called back, after three or four days, his reaction to our sponsorship deal was surprisingly cool. Portugal sounded like a great destination, but he dismissed a June trip out of hand; there wasn't enough time to get the boat ready. Besides, he said, he was planning a major climbing trip in Central Asia with friends in July and a June voyage would conflict with his training. Why couldn't we go in August?

On my cell phone thousands of miles away, I couldn't believe what I was hearing! I had just lined up thousands of dollars in sponsorship to send the boat to Portugal, and this was his reaction? That the trip conflicted with his vacation plans?

I struggled to keep my rage in check, but the argument escalated. Again Garth complained that the boat was always moving ahead on my schedule. My schedule? It's our sponsor's schedule, I answered. The boat *must* be there in June. In an all-too-familiar replay of our earlier battles, we dredged up old arguments and lingering resentments.

Our dispute continued over a couple of days and several phone calls. In the end, though, Garth gave in. "I guess I can go climbing another year," he said. But when I got back to Washington the next week, he wasn't there. He had slipped away for a substitute trip, though one closer to home. Peeved, I headed over to the Boat Works to assess our situation.

As I walked up the alley, I saw the lady with the big jaw approaching, the one who had always greeted me cheerfully as I sorted corks, alone, in the garage. She was on one of her daily walks.

"Hiya, Buddy! How's the big"—she paused, searching for the right word—"thing?"

"It's great!" I answered. "In fact, we're taking it to Portugal!"

When I reached the garage, Harold was across the alley, leaning over the engine of his car, wrench in hand. "Hey! It's really great to see you!" he said. "How was your trip?"

I hadn't seen him since returning from Antarctica. "Cold," I said. "I had a great time. But the big news is that we have sponsorship for the boat! Cork Supply is shipping the boat to Portugal, and we're going down the Douro River! Can you believe it?"

Harold nodded. "I always had faith in you."

"You should come along," I said. "Really. You helped build the boat, as much as anyone. You should come. It's going to be fun."

"Thanks, but I can't," he said. His daughter still had two more years of college; a big trip abroad would have to wait.

And Harold had bad news to report. "The old man died," he said. Mac, the skeptical taxi driver, had just passed away. Sure enough, his station wagon was gone; even the oil stain on the alley's rough pavement looked a little faint.

Mac had never "gotten" the boat. And we hadn't talked much after I tried, once or twice, to explain the concept to him. Some of his friends hadn't quite understood it, either. In the fall, one of them had asked me, in all seriousness, if I intended to sail the *Cork Boat* on my "trip to the North Pole."

"No," I answered, truthfully. North Pole, South Pole, I knew what she meant. "I don't think it would survive the ice."

The boat, though, snug in its berth, had survived the mild Washington winter in perfect shape. If we grafted a few more hexagonal cork disks onto the misaligned bow log (to avoid insulting the Portuguese), the hull would be good to go. The deck, sail, oars, and steering systems were another matter. Our test launch in the Potomac had shown them all to be virtually useless.

When Garth returned, he got to work designing a bigger, more robust, three-part deck system, mainly to accommodate new oars, a bigger centerboard, and a new rudder. I focused on adapting our existing mast to carry a new, bigger sail—a square sail, more in keeping with the style of traditional Douro riverboats, which I had researched online.

Under the gun once again, Garth and I worked well together, playing off each other's strengths. If we didn't always reach decisions easily, the final results were always better for our having hashed them out. Only my insistence on having a sail continued to cause a flap.

"It's not a sailboat," Garth insisted. "It's an oar rig."

"We're not building a rowboat!" I said. While I was willing

to concede that oars would probably be our primary means of propulsion, apart from the river's current, I also knew the joys and benefits of sailing. Garth, who was not a sailor, didn't. The more we could harness the wind, I said, the less we'd have to bust our tails rowing. Besides, a sail would look good.

He held his ground. Deep down, I knew that our visions for the boat weren't that different, but we had both become invested in the argument, defending our respective positions. This particular design dispute had become, like so many others, a proxy for the broader clash of ego and personality. Fueled by lingering resentment on both sides, it went on for a couple of days.

"I know more about building than you do," he said, reiterating a point he had made before. "I've worked in an architect's office for four years, and I resent you issuing orders from on high."

Orders? I was the one who had collected the corks, put in the most hours of drudgery, kept the project moving forward, and secured thousands of dollars in sponsorship for a trip to Portugal. I wasn't issuing orders; but I felt I had earned the right to assert myself, at least on the margins.

"This isn't an either-or situation," I said, trying to steer a middle course. "We should have both oars *and* a sail, just like the Vikings." My stubbornness, and my appeal to his keen sense of aesthetics, finally won the day.

In Annapolis, back at Bacon Sails, we met a sailmaker named Tara Quinn. She loved the project from the start, and once she figured out that we weren't, in her words, "a couple of trust-funders," she agreed to sew our sail at cost: just $200, plus materials.

We were relieved. The previous fall, we had quickly come to understand the old saying that "a boat is just a hole in the water to throw money into." Even with free corks and free labor, the boat had cost us $6,000 to get into the water the first time. Getting it ready and fitted out for Portugal was looking like another four grand. But there was no other way.

As Garth started building the new decks in a borrowed basement woodshop a few blocks from the Boat Works, I started dealing with the paperwork and bureaucracy associated with the trip. Getting the boat licensed, shipping it to Portugal, clearing customs, and acquiring the proper permits for the river trip would take time. My contact at Cork Supply Portugal had e-mailed me a list of additional requirements. Apparently, engineers from the Portuguese navy would have to inspect the boat in Lisbon to certify its seaworthiness. Did I have blueprints for the boat? Could I send my local boat registration? And could I please forward a copy of my sailor's license?

Blueprints? A sailor's license? A naval inspection in Lisbon? The best I could do was send some of Garth's diagrams from his application to architecture school; I also picked up the textbook for the Red Cross Sailing Certificate—the exam was multiple choice. When I presented the project to the Portuguese Embassy, officials there promised to help. The military attaché, it turned out, was a Portuguese admiral. He agreed to make a few calls "to exert some pressure" about skipping the inspection, as soon as he was done arranging the Washington visit of the Portuguese defense minister.

As our shipping deadline neared, it became apparent that the decks might not be done in time. Or, rather, *would* not be done in time. I pressed Garth—working away in that dim, basement woodshop, with its seven-foot ceiling hung with pipes—to hurry. He got angry. Didn't I understand that the decks took time? It was the same conflict, over and over again. What could I do? Garth would do a perfect job, but on his schedule, not mine. I called the shipper's agent and asked if we could send the boat in the forty-foot shipping container, as planned, but air-freight the decks, mast, and oars a couple weeks later. My contact said that sending the mast air freight would be difficult, given its length. But she was a fan of the *Cork Boat* and would see what she could do.

She also warned me that European Union authorities were getting very strict concerning agricultural imports. Hearing this, my thoughts raced to the boat—it was one giant agricultural import. But that wasn't what she meant. If I intended to ship anything on wooden pallets, she explained, the pallets would have to be certified; apparently, certain voracious beetles had taken a liking to pine in all its forms, and the EU didn't want them hitching a free ride to the Continent. I scribbled down "find plastic pallets" on my growing to-do list.

I called Salah, our favorite trucker, about getting the boat up to Baltimore. The ship that would transport our boat to Portugal was sailing from the port there. No problem, Salah said; but with mileage, it would probably cost another $200. On the appointed day, he came rumbling up the alley with his truck. This time, we loaded the boat in less than twenty minutes. We were getting good at this.

"We have to make one stop on the way," I told Salah. "The D.C. Harbor Patrol. They have to inspect the boat." Unfortunately, there was no way out of this one. In order to clear customs in Portugal, I needed to send them, in advance, a copy of the boat's title and registration. And in order to obtain these, the boat, being a home-built vessel, had to pass inspection with the D.C. Harbor Patrol.

I wasn't looking forward to it. If there was one bureaucracy I feared more than the Portuguese Customs Ministry, it was that of the District of Columbia. Having endured interminable delays registering my car at the District's Soviet-style Department of Motor Vehicles, I knew that its irritable, obstructionist, bureaucratic dissemblers could make—indeed, enjoyed making—life miserable for all those who passed within the faintest shadow of their authority.

And we had to get the *Cork Boat* to Baltimore immediately. The *Ideal,* the only ship heading from the United States to Portugal that would arrive in time to meet our deadline, wasn't going to wait for late cargo, especially a boat made of corks. If the Harbor Patrol didn't give the boat a passing grade the first time—right now—we were sunk.

The Harbor Patrol is located down on the Potomac, not far from the fish market. I knew exactly where it was, having made three previous trips there to provide the officials with documentation on the boat. I tried to think positive. Maybe my several earlier visits there had been of value, a chance to build a constructive relationship. Maybe they'd be sympathetic.

We rumbled up with the boat, and I went inside to summon the officer on duty. Walking out to the boat, he told me he had been working for ten hours straight and was leaving shortly to pick up relatives at the airport. I didn't know what to think: Would he be in a hurry to give the boat a rubber-stamp yes so he could get going? Or would he be cranky from his long shift?

Feigning nonchalance, I gave him a few quiet moments to wrap his eyes around our unusual, twenty-two-foot craft. Strapped to the back of Salah's truck, it looked even bigger and stranger than usual. At eye level, I could see the bottom of the boat. A couple of the trinity lashings had come loose, but I couldn't do anything about that now.

"All cork?" Officer Carter asked. "Solid Cork!" I answered, giving the boat's flank a confident slap. For once, I omitted the fact that the boat consisted of 165,321 separate corks, 15,000 rubber bands, and not a drop of glue.

"Well," he observed, "it isn't going to *sink*."

There was a hint of hesitation in his voice, almost as if he were asking a question. In all honesty, I had my own doubts. Sink? No. Break apart into thousands of pieces? Maybe.

"No sir, that's for sure. It's not going to sink."

"Well, I guess you're okay then," he announced, suddenly and firmly, having made his decision. Officer Carter was giving us a passing grade. After fetching the paperwork from his office, we headed on north, toward Baltimore.

As we drove, I asked Salah what he thought of his cargo. He was accustomed to hauling special loads, he said. Once it was a speedboat for a Saudi prince. Another time it was a French troop truck being converted for use as an RV. Just a few weeks earlier, he had been called to a private home for what he thought would be a run-of-the-mill towing job. When the owner opened his garage door, there was a gleaming, mint-condition, royal-blue 1929 Rolls-Royce convertible inside, complete with a vintage wicker picnic basket strapped to the running board. "That one I loaded very carefully," he said.

Turning off the expressway, we passed through the grim, industrial flats surrounding the Port of Baltimore. It was the kind of landscape where, if you bulldozed away the construction debris, you might find the lost molars of Jimmy Hoffa. Arriving at a dark, cavernous warehouse filled with pallets of slabbed marble, we tracked down the boss. A heavy man in a blue suit, he looked like somebody straight out of a mob movie—complete with fresh stitching from heart surgery peeking through his open collar. He promised to take good care of our boat.

As we rolled it off Salah's truck onto the loading dock, forty dolly wheels squealed and skidded across the concrete. Garth said it sounded "like a flock of seagulls accompanied by whale-song." It felt strange to leave it in that big warehouse, unprotected. But Salah had other runs, and we had to get back to Washington. So we snapped a few quick pictures for posterity and bid our boat bon voyage.

The final ten days passed in a blur of sawdust, research on the river, midnight runs to Home Depot, the sharp smell of polyurethane, and too many shopping trips to Annapolis. As I was leaving Bacon Sails for the last time, one of the new sales-men caught up with me in the parking lot. He had heard about the *Cork Boat* from his colleagues, and wanted to talk.

His name was Brendan Lake. A native of Maine, he'd built his own twenty-four-foot wooden boat at the age of nineteen and, three years later, sailed it all the way to Florida. He had some advice for me: Be open to people along the way. "You'll find that a lot of people are ready to help you when you arrive in an unusual craft," he said. "An old man once gave me a sixty-foot ketch because he liked my boat." With that, and some parting advice on sailing a square-rigged boat, he wished me well.

It all sounded incredibly romantic, but at that moment I was actually more concerned with finding plastic pallets that would pass the EU beetle inspection. Working both the Yellow Pages and the Web, I discovered that they were not so afford-able or easy to come by—at least not in quantities of two.

Finally, I discovered that the U.S. Postal Service used plastic pallets for bulk mail shipments, and that I might be able to "borrow" a few from one of their big processing facilities on the outskirts of Washington. So the day before our shipping deadline, Phil Guire drove me over there in his SUV. Paranoid about anthrax, however, which had recently killed two postal employees and shut down one of its facilities completely, the Postal Service had beefed up its security.

"Without authorization, I can't let you even enter, let alone leave, with Postal Service property," the guard at the gate insisted. But after I described the *Cork Boat* to her—or maybe because a huge downpour was rolling toward us—she finally relented. "Just don't tell me any more, or I'll have to report you two loonies," she said, waving us through the gate. We had our plastic pallets.

Garth scored a similar victory—four free oars—by chatting up the rowing coach at a popular Georgetown boathouse, down on the Potomac. "Can you back your car in here and make it quick?" the coach had asked, casting a nervous glance to see if anyone was watching. Twelve feet long, the oars stuck out of his car's passenger window like a bundle of jousting lances. But we got them back to the Boat Works, and only scraped one parked car in the process.

True to form, we ran out of time, and Garth and I had to pull another all-nighter to get the air-freight shipment ready. There were no volunteers to help this time. As Garth worked fast and furious in the woodshop a few blocks away, I renewed my old acquaintance with the garage floor as I strapped our completed decks to the shipping pallets and wrapped them in old carpeting to protect them from gouges and scratches. At one point I took a short break, and returned to see a stray cat pissing all over the carpet. Yelling, I chased it from the garage, which now stunk to high heaven. I soon learned that duct tape doesn't stick well to piss-soaked carpet, and had to work around those spots.

Throughout the night, I kept a nervous eye on the alley. A visitor had been held up at gunpoint just a few days earlier, right in front of Garth's house. Our Boat Works didn't seem quite so safe anymore, especially as the hour grew late. Sometime after two A.M., I ran out of duct tape altogether, and started using string. It was that kind of night.

At eight-thirty A.M., a weary Garth carried over the last of our three decks, and I sprayed on a quick coat of polyurethane, the roar of our compressor breaking the morning peace. I hoped the sun would dry it by nine-thirty, when Salah was due to arrive with his truck.

And the rudder? Garth hadn't even had time to start it. He would have to bring it with him, as carry-on.

Together, Garth and I made sure we had packed everything into the shipment—spools of webbing, come-alongs, surplus netting, Dacron line, life jackets, coils of extra rope, a first-aid kit, miscellaneous tools, pulleys, and cleats for the deck rigging, river maps, waterproof matches, a few fistfuls of rubber bands—anything and everything we might need to operate or repair the boat on the river.

At ten-thirty, I phoned Salah to find out where he was—he was never late. He said his truck had broken down but would be fixed "soon." Meanwhile, one of Garth's neighbors backed out of his garage without looking and ran over our mast with his gas-guzzling SUV. Fortunately, the mast was okay. My packaging job had saved it—or maybe it was the lucky cat piss. In any case, the clock was ticking.

When Salah finally showed up, just before noon, Garth and I helped him load the truck as quickly as we could, then climbed up into the cab. "Salah, it never ends, does it?" I said, handing him the address of the air-freight company. "It's going out to Dulles, and Garth's going along to make sure the shipment gets off okay. But would you mind dropping me at Dupont Circle?"

A block from my apartment, I climbed out of the truck's cab and waved a quick goodbye as it rolled off down Connecticut Avenue. Then I hurried home, hair greasy, face unshaven, pants torn, T-shirt ruined, and hands still gunked up and sticky with polyurethane. The last week had taken its toll, and I was a wreck. But there was no time to relax or recuperate. I had ninety minutes to shower, pack, and get to the airport. I had a flight to catch, too.

LAND OF MAGELLAN

A t the Porto airport, a disinterested customs official glanced at my passport, looked up at me, and asked the nature of my visit to Portugal. "Business or holiday?"

Neither, I thought to myself. This definitely wasn't a business trip. But it certainly wasn't a vacation, either. A vacation is supposed to be easy and relaxing, and the *Cork Boat* was anything but. In fact, what was once a boyhood dream had somehow stirred up such a maelstrom of sweat, hope, anger, joy, frustration, and excitement that my trip to Portugal felt more like vindication than anything else.

"Holiday," I said. He stamped my passport and waved me through.

Exiting customs into the airport lobby, I spotted a man with curly brown hair holding up a MR. POLLACK sign. I took a deep breath—it was show time.

The man was Jorge Osório, my contact at Cork Supply Portugal. We had exchanged dozens of e-mails in the weeks before the boat shipped, and all the headaches we had shared made for a familiar greeting. Also there to greet me was his boss, Francisco Pinto, the company's European sales manager.

Both were alive with optimism and excitement, and glad to finally meet "the man behind the boat." We sat down at the airport café for a quick coffee and they updated me on the boat's status. Rough weather in the Atlantic had delayed our ship, Francisco said, so the *Cork Boat* had not yet arrived. It was due any day, and we would worry then about getting it through customs.

"How long do you think that will take?" I asked. Having invited my parents, cousins, and other friends to celebrate the launch in about a week, I was eager to stick to schedule.

"It once took me six months to clear a half-dozen bottles of imported wine," Francisco answered. "Either it will be very simple or a big problem."

He had checked into river conditions, too. The rains had been light this year, so the water would be relatively calm; no whitewater. I thought instantly of Sara's death. To me, rivers always seemed a little dangerous, whitewater or not.

Even apart from my personal experience, Garth and I had talked with concern about the potential for rapids. The boat was only as strong as its net sheathing. Rip that open on a sharp rock and our beloved craft would start hemorrhaging corks by the thousand.

Yes, the water was calm, Francisco continued. Maybe too calm. Because of the drought, the Dam Authority wasn't letting much water through the dams. I knew from my research that there were five dams on the Douro between Spain and Porto. Characteristically, my dad had found an obscure website entitled "Large Dams in Portugal," and so I had stats and photos on every one we would pass. All were enormous, but they did have locks to permit boat traffic. I would need to make arrangements with the Dam Authority to pass through each of them in turn.

But that was part of the adventure. Francisco held up his arm and flexed. "You're going to arrive in Porto with huge biceps!" he said, laughing.

Driving into Porto from the airport, we passed Leixões, the city's port. Giant cranes were loading and unloading container after container from waiting cargo ships. This weird, spindly flock of birdlike machines looked something like a group of mechanical storks, and I hoped that they would soon be delivering the *Cork Boat,* safe and sound.

As we left the expressway and started up through the crowded, cobbled streets of the old city, a stoplight brought us to a halt in front of a small neighborhood cinema, shuttered and closed. I didn't even need Portuguese to read the faded, tattered posters; they told their story in a single word: *Titanic.*

Porto, an ancient hilly city of nearly a million people, had clearly seen better centuries. But the pealing bells of ornate churches, the red-tiled garrets overlooking narrow twisted lanes, the tidy shops and balconies fluttering with laundry, even the great, grimy steel bridges over the Douro itself— all of these lent the city an air of enduring grace. If its cuffs were a little frayed, Porto still carried itself with dignity. And deservedly so.

For fifteen centuries, it had been home in turn to Romans, Vandals, Christians, Moors, Crusaders, navigators, French soldiers, British merchants, and Portuguese revolutionaries. The very name Portugal, I had learned, was derived from the Latin word for "port," *portus*, and the name of the settlement across the river during that era, Cale. And while Lisbon had been shaken to the ground in the great earthquake of 1755, Porto stood strong. Jorge informed me that proud residents liked to call it "The Invincible City."

My hotel, perched high on a hill, offered a commanding view of the city. My window looked out over a panorama of jumbled rooftops, all the way across the Douro to Vila Nova de Gaia, the city where all the famous "port lodges" age their wine. Apart from a medieval cathedral crowning a neighboring hilltop, the best part of my view were all the seagulls soaring about. Apparently, there were thermals that rolled up the hillside from the river below, and these birds rode them upwards effortlessly, picking up speed, soaring into the sky until—just outside my window—they paused, wheeled, and dove again.

I ate alone that night at an old beaux arts–style restaurant, the Café Majestic, not far from my hotel. Lined with aging mirrors, hung with chandeliers, and adorned with plaster cherubs, the place appeared as if it hadn't changed a bit since its opening as a private club in 1921. To celebrate my arrival in the land of navigators, I savored a glass of thirty-year-old port—aged, appropriately, the precise number of years I had been saving corks. "Cheers," I said to myself, only a little bit lonely. "This is going to be the grandest of adventures."

As usual, there was a lot to get done. After a day of rest and wandering, I met up with Francisco, who had arranged a series of meetings. The first was with Olga Sousa, the public relations agent whom Cork Supply had hired to promote the boat. Focused, friendly, and professional, she had lost no time in getting started: I was already scheduled for an interview that afternoon with *Espresso*, Portugal's leading weekly.

The interview, in English, seemed to go well enough. My story was simple: Fulfilling a boyhood dream, I had saved corks for thirty years to build a boat. Now I had brought that boat to Portugal for a trip down the mighty Douro.

The reporter's questions were simple. Why Portugal? Why the Douro?

I replied that Portugal was the king of cork, exporting more cork than any other country in the world; that the Douro region was known worldwide both for its beauty and its wine; and that Portugal had produced some of history's greatest navigators—Magellan, Cabral, and Vasco da Gama. Finally, I noted that our sponsor, the Cork Supply Group, was based in Portugal. How could we celebrate the *Cork Boat*'s maiden voyage anywhere else?

Was I an engineer? No. But I had built the boat with my friend Garth Goldstein, an architect. Garth would be arriving in a few days, and we would travel down the river together, along with family and friends. We would be sailing from the village of Barca de Alva, on the Spanish border, all the way to Porto, where the river meets the sea.

And what does Bill Clinton think of the boat? Did he supply any of the corks? Olga had told the reporter that I was a former Presidential speechwriter.

I answered that I couldn't speak for my former boss, but that the boat did include corks from the *Casa Branca*—the White House. I added that in addition to all the corks donated by Cork Supply, thousands of people in the United States had given corks for the boat, and that every cork represented a memory or a dream. There were a lot of people traveling with us, in spirit.

"It is a boat of dreams," I said. "Everybody has dreams."

Olga had advised me beforehand to mention one specific concern: I told the reporter that everybody in Portugal had been so friendly and helpful, but that I only hoped customs officials would not hold the boat up when it arrived. It was a subtle, preemptive dig at the unpopular Customs Ministry. Although my comment would probably make them angry, it would also put them on the spot. With the public eager to see this so-called cork boat, they wouldn't be as likely to drag out the clearance process, or levy exorbitant taxes.

And then it was time for the photo shoot. In the absence of the boat itself, which was still at sea, we decided to do it out at the Cork Supply factory, in a little village near Porto called Santa Maria de Lamas. It reminded me of their California plant—the conveyor belts, the ink machines, the women sorting corks.

I was psyched to finally see something I'd never seen before: raw cork. It came in great rough, curving sheets, cut by hatchet from the trunks of cork oak trees. A short, mustachioed man with a chain-mail glove was feeding these sheets, one by one, into a very hungry saw blade. Moments after being cut, the sheets passed under an automatic stamping machine that punched out corks by the dozens. The leftover cork bark, looking something like Swiss cheese, was then carried away on a conveyor belt, to be ground up for other uses. It was like visiting Willy Wonka's chocolate factory, but instead of making Gobstoppers the machines made bottle stoppers.

The photographer, accustomed to shooting royalty and business tycoons and society weddings, wasn't impressed. Though I'd been told he was one of the best in the country, I had my doubts. He had a greasy comb-over, a bulging gut, and a well-worn suit that was a size too small. As I posed in front of bales of cork and—at his direction—vamped in giant cork bins like a swimsuit model in khakis, I was a little ill at ease. I knew it would probably be good PR for the boat, but I wasn't comfortable in front of the camera. I could only smile and hope that his sartorial tastes were no reflection of his photographic skills.

A few hours later Olga's phone was ringing off the hook. Somehow, Portugal's top dailies had gotten wind of *Espresso*'s scoop, and they wanted interviews, too.

Back at the hotel, I called Garth to give him an update and get his arrival information. Things were moving fast here, I said. He should get to Porto as soon as possible.

His report was grim. The owner of the woodshop was having marital difficulties and the metallic whine of the circular saw was upsetting his wife. She wanted peace and quiet after ten P.M., a restriction that had been cutting into his construction schedule. The rudder, which he was redesigning to meet airline baggage requirements, was still not done. The sail, too, was problematic. While our sailmaker had completed it on time, Garth had learned that hiring a professional to silk-screen the Cork Supply logo onto it would cost us $800. To save the money, he had decided to scan the logo on his home computer and print out special, iron-on transfers. But the transfer sheets, designed for cotton T-shirts, weren't sticking well to the synthetic sailcloth.

Oh, and he hadn't bought a ticket yet.

My blood pressure surged. Construction problems were inevitable. But procrastinating on travel plans? That was risky:

it was peak tourist season, and flights were hard to come by. I tried to contain my anger, because I was stuck. If absolutely necessary, I could make the trip without Garth, but I couldn't make it without the rudder and sail. I thought angrily about his recent ten-day climbing trip, but said nothing. I could only fume.

"We're still on target to launch in seven or eight days, customs permitting," I said, trying to conceal my aggravation. "So the sooner you can get here, the better."

Even as I seethed over his absence, though, I felt a little guilty. There he was, slaving away in Washington, while I was having a good time in Portugal. Sure, I was hustling; but I was having a lot of fun, too. For the past week I had been eating exceptionally well—crispy local sardines, enormous tiger shrimp, tender grilled octopus, and delicious *arroz de marisco*—all compliments of Cork Supply.

The following night would be no exception. Once again, the Cork Supply team took me out on the town with a group of visiting clients, high-end vintners from California to whom they had wanted to show the boat. We went to a raucous Brazilian restaurant, where a dreadlocked guitar player sang *bossa nova* as a crowd of waiters carved various succulent meats straight off swords and onto our plates until we begged them to stop.

The *caipirinhas* and wine flowed, too. At one point, I counted upwards of ninety glasses on the table—for a party of sixteen. After things got a little rowdy and several glasses smashed to the floor, people calmed down, and we switched to a bottle of 1963 port. Then we were all off to the disco. Throughout the evening, I kept thinking to myself: All this, from the *Cork Boat*? All those miserable hours, all the doubt, and all the work were suddenly paying dividends I had never imagined.

I got up a little late the next day, feeling hungover. Unfortunately, there was work to do. My main project for the day was a meeting Francisco had arranged for me at Douro Azul, the leading riverboat company that ran big tourist boats up and down the Douro. I hoped to learn more about the river, and to enlist their support for the boat and its journey.

The taxi let me off in front of a picturesque stone building on a sunny esplanade overlooking the river. It had heavy, ten-foot doors, glossy with layer after layer of paint. Inside, the floors sloped and crooked beams held up dubious ceilings of peeling paint. Its thick stone walls, probably centuries old, were decorated with *azulejos*—traditional, hand-painted blue tiles—depicting the *barcos rabelos*, port boats, being pulled along by oxen on a riverside towpath. Following the directions I'd been given, I made my way up a creaky, twisting staircase to the second floor, in search of the Douro Azul office.

Pedro Negrão, the company's manager, looked about forty. He had, he said, grown up with Francisco Pinto's younger brother. After listening to my pitch, which I made mostly in English but embellished with the Portuguese I had been studying in spare moments, Negrão said he liked the idea of the *Cork Boat*, and would instruct his captains to assist us.

"We like to support the river," he said, adding that our boat, by generating interest in the Douro, would promote the tourism that was his company's lifeblood. He said he would also speak with people at the Dam Authority on our behalf; he hoped they would be lenient about lock times.

"Perhaps, though it is forbidden, they will let you keep the boat in the locks overnight. There, it will be safe," he said. Otherwise, we ought to post a watch.

One of his captains, a former merchant marine named Hugo, reviewed the maps I had brought and recommended some stopping points. You will be doing a lot of rowing, he warned. The current is very slow.

Afterward, striding through the streets on my way back to the hotel, I felt great. Logistics were shaping up. The journey clearly promised challenges, but planning and preparing for them was turning out to be a lot of fun.

All these errands reminded me of passages from Alan Moorehead's book *The White Nile* in which he describes the great African explorers and their extensive preparations in Cairo and in Zanzibar before setting off into the wilds of Africa. And I also thought of Shackleton, down in Buenos Aires, finalizing arrangements for his fateful, doomed trip into the Antarctic.

The Norwegian adventurer Thor Heyerdahl had also written of the many logistical nightmares he and his party had encountered while preparing for the *Kon-Tiki* expedition across the Pacific. Heyerdahl, coincidentally, had just died, at the age of eighty-seven, having survived both storms of the sea and of life. I had loved his book as a boy, in my early boat-building days. It seemed a fitting tribute now to be launching a boat that he had helped inspire.

Of course, the voyage of the *Cork Boat* would be nowhere near as dangerous as the journeys that Heyerdahl or the others had undertaken in their day. Nor would it carry any special historical significance. But it was still an adventure. Even my Portuguese hosts were intrigued by this most unusual boat, and the journey that lay before it.

A few days later, I called Garth to check in again. He was still in rudder hell, making repeated, midnight runs out to Home Depot. And if that weren't bad enough, someone had broken into the Boat Works and stolen the air compressor we'd borrowed to stain the decks. That would probably cost us a couple hundred dollars to replace. More worrisome, he reported that he wouldn't be arriving for another four days.

I could only make the best of it. I told Garth that the boat would probably be coming out of customs the day he arrived. With luck, we still might make our revised launch date, the following weekend. "Just get here," I urged him, trying not to order—or to beg. "We're running out of time."

As we hung up, something didn't seem right. My intuition

was correct. Garth called back a few minutes later, very upset. He didn't like the way I was setting the schedule. He felt it was too rigid.

"This is my summer vacation," he said. "I want to play it by ear. I don't want to rush."

I resisted the urge to hang up on him. The project had become too big and too complex and involved too many people just to "play it by ear." Besides, time management wasn't Garth's forte; if I let him set our schedule, the boat might never even make it onto the river, let alone back to Porto. But I held my tongue.

"I'm totally willing to change our schedule as conditions warrant," I reassured him. "But I'm not willing to start out with no schedule at all."

Again, we both hung up angry. Why was there so much conflict, I wondered, in a project that was supposed to be fun?

The next morning, the story of the boat hit the newsstands—big national stories that, for all their misspellings and small errors, really captured the spirit of the boat and its impending journey. The fact that there were no pictures of the boat itself, I now realized, would only pique people's curiosity. The headlines were great: AMERICAN TO DESCEND DOURO IN CORK BOAT—COLLECTED CORKS SINCE HE WAS SEVEN, and THE CORKSCREW—CLINTON ADVISOR BUILDS BOAT OF 160,000 CORKS, WILL DESCEND DOURO.

Editors, although primarily taken with the idea of a boyhood dream fulfilled, had also seized on the Clinton angle.

I hadn't made a big deal about my old job, or claimed to be a friend or close advisor of the President, but for all the Portuguese press cared, I had been one of Bill Clinton's top aides. I felt bad for Garth, whose name was barely mentioned, but if he wasn't here, how were reporters going to interview him?

Pushing those thoughts aside, I piled a stack of extra papers into the backseat of Jorge's car, and we headed out of Porto and up the river for a scouting run. We wanted to see what river conditions were like, and check out some of the dams. Over the past several days, we had been spending a lot of time together, and I had come to admire his spirit of can-do optimism. Being a kayaker and a cork salesman, but most of all a romantic, he had become very passionate about the *Cork Boat,* making its success in Portugal his personal mission.

A few hours later, we pulled into Peso da Régua, a regional center about two hours east of Porto, where we stopped for coffee at a street-side café. Spotting a free table, I squeezed past two men studying a newspaper, and saying something about a *"barco de rolhas."* Wait—I knew those words! They meant "cork boat." Glancing back, I spotted my picture, and a headline about the boat.

"Jorge," I said, cocking my head toward the two men, "those guys are talking about the boat!" Jorge didn't waste a moment. He got up, walked back over to the men's table, and, laughing, pointed me out. "There's the man building the *Cork Boat,*" he said. A little embarrassed by the sudden attention, I took off my sunglasses and nodded modestly in acknowledgment. Curious, they motioned me over.

Earlier, in the car, Jorge had given me a warning. "You're going to have to speak Portuguese upriver," he said. "They won't speak English." He had spent the past hour and a half helping me convert my fluent Spanish into basic, functional Portuguese. But if I had harbored any flickering illusions about my new linguistic proficiency, they were snuffed out by the fire hose of language that suddenly blasted forth from these two men. As they pumped my hand in congratulations and fired questions at me, all I could do was smile, nod, and look desperately to Jorge for translation.

"You are very fortunate, my friend," Jorge said. "Only last month, these gentlemen formed a new organization called the Association of Friends of the Douro River. They want to help you with your journey, because you, too, are a friend of the Douro."

Jorge always spoke poetically, at least in English, which was one of four languages he spoke fluently. And if he had good news to report, his speech acquired an especially joyful, rhythmic lilt. This was great news.

Ten minutes later, we were down on the stone quay by the river, surrounded by a dozen Friends of the Douro. Soon we were introduced to Francisco Lopez, deputy director of the Dam Authority—precisely the man who could swiftly authorize our passage through the locks. I couldn't quite believe my luck, and told him I was looking forward to seeing his dams.

I got my first look at one an hour later when Jorge and I drove out of Régua and on up the river. Though I'd seen a photo on the "Large Dams in Portugal" website, it hadn't prepared me for the real thing—a sheer wall of concrete rising up, up, up. I gulped.

"That's big," I said.

Jorge laughed. "You are going to have a true adventure, my friend!"

Later that day, in a small riverside town called Pinhão, we stopped for a drink at the Vintage House. Built from a converted port lodge, this elegant, high-ceilinged hotel of stone and old beams was a monument to British colonialism that would have inspired even Kipling. Draped in bougainvillea and furnished in high colonial style with deep armchairs, leather-bound books, fine Oriental carpets, and gilt-framed oils of nineteenth-century gentlemen, it was so tastefully done that it made me think of Marlene. In fact, I noticed a sofa upholstered in the same striped silk that she had used to re-cover one of her chairs at the bed-and-breakfast. The place was perfect.

I was particularly enchanted by an oversized, antique map of the river, framed on the wall. Yellowed, water-stained, and missing a corner, it must have been twelve feet long. Its title, set in flourishing type in both English and Portuguese, read: "The Navigable Douro River and Its Tributaries, from

Madrid to the Atlantic Ocean." It had been published by the Royal Geographic Society in 1858, and its detailed meanderings stirred my hunger for the voyage ahead. Soon, I would be making that same journey, or part of it, joining the stream of history from Spain to the sea.

The Douro, I was learning, had been a dangerous river for most of its history. In ancient times, it had been known as "the river of bad navigation." Just the previous year, Jorge said, surging floods had washed out a highway bridge just as a bus was crossing over it. The bus had plunged over the precipice and into the water, drowning all fifty-seven people aboard. Even though we would not be traveling in flood season, the story struck a nerve. I could empathize with those who had lost loved ones to the river, more keenly than Jorge could possibly know.

In the late afternoon, before driving back to Porto, Jorge and I hired a motor launch to take us out on the river. The wind was blowing hard, from the east, and kicking up whitecaps. I asked Valdemar, our barefoot boatman, if this was typical weather. I wasn't sure if the *Cork Boat* could make headway against headwinds this strong.

"It always blows from the sea," he answered. "The winds from Spain we call *Los Gallegos*—from Galicia."

"When do those come?" I asked, hopefully. Catching *Los Gallegos* would make our trip a whole lot easier.

"Not until the fall," he said. "And even then, not very often."

———

The next day, my seventh in Portugal, was Sunday. I decided to follow local tradition and make it a day of rest. Tired of hustling, I was grateful when Francisco invited me to his country house for the day, about an hour outside of Porto. Approaching from a rutted lane overhung with grapevines, I was expecting a pretty little cottage. What I found was a rugged, four-hundred-year-old walled manor, built of huge granite blocks and hand-hewn beams, graced with a gurgling fountain in its sunny courtyard. Although plain in its architecture, it was, nevertheless, magnificent. Francisco was modest. "It was practically a ruin when I bought it eleven years ago," he said. "There wasn't even a road here."

He had worried about his kids spending too much time in the big city, and about the temptations they might face as teenagers. A weekend house was the perfect solution. "This way we can spend time together, as a family. The kids can have their friends out. And I can keep a few cows, some geese, and pretend I'm a farmer."

Over a cold beer, he told me the story of the house, a story that seemed to capture a lot about modern Portugal. Although we weren't far from a big, modern city, and despite the fact that over eighty percent of Portuguese carry a cell phone (two if they're young and hip), old ideas and attitudes died hard.

He had bought the house for a modest sum from an old

man who, at the outset of long and slow negotiations, said he would sell only on one condition: no paperwork and no banks. The man had once had a bad experience with a bank. After his sister had died, the bank told him it had closed her account and transferred the balance to a new one under his name. But how could this be? He hadn't seen them move any money. In fact, he had never seen the money at all. The bank was clearly trying to pull a fast one. Angry and suspicious, the old man insisted on seeing the actual money. Weary of the dispute and sensitive to the suspicions of an older, less sophisticated generation, the bank ultimately sent an armored car filled with cash to the village. Nevertheless, he didn't want to deal with a bank this time.

Over the course of many months, Francisco convinced him that, despite his past experience, a bank really was necessary. Francisco suggested they all go down to the bank together, so he could see the money change hands. Though still suspicious of banks and bankers, the old man was eager to sell the property, and he agreed. On the appointed day, he showed up at the bank with two witnesses—another sister and her neighbor. In a private office, the banker presented him with several stacks of banknotes worth tens of thousands of dollars—the exact sum of the sale. Bill by bill, the old man began to count his money.

After about twenty minutes, the man was still counting his way through the first stack of cash. The banker, growing impatient, blurted out, "Don't worry, the machine already counted it."

Looking up at the banker from the stack of crisp banknotes, the old man answered dryly, "And so far it hasn't made a mistake." Two hours later, he walked out of the bank, a big plastic garbage bag stuffed with money over his shoulder.

"Who knows where he put it?" Francisco said. "Maybe he buried it."

Although Portugal, which had gotten billions in development aid from the European Union, was changing fast, his little country home was still a retreat into a simpler past. Occasionally, on the local roads, he still saw oxen pulling home-built carts that rolled along on axles greased with pig fat. "You can hear them coming, it makes a song," he said, closing his eyes and starting to hum. Francisco loved his country, in all its tradition and all its promise.

After lunch, he brought out a yellowed, thumb-worn copy of *Kon-Tiki*, a Portuguese translation. "I had this book as a boy," he said, putting his hand on the shoulder of his own twelve-year-old son, who sat next to him on the couch. "This is very appropriate, no?"

Then he began to read, in perfect English: "Once in a while you find yourself in an odd situation. You get into it by degrees and in the most natural way but, when you are right in the midst of it, you are suddenly astonished and ask yourself how in the world it all came about. If, for example, you put to sea on a wooden raft with a parrot and five companions . . ."

Francisco looked up and smiled. Yes, he understood the *Cork Boat*. And we understood each other.

Late Monday, Jorge called to say the air-freight shipment—our decks, oars, and mast—had been released from customs, and would be delivered to Global Quality Control, Cork Supply's test facility in Rio Meão, a small village not far from Porto. Global, as it was called within the company, had a warehouse in which we could assemble the boat.

When we arrived, the entire staff was busy mopping out the building. A pipe had broken over the weekend, flooding the entire facility. Ironically, the air shipment—decks, life jackets, and other assorted boat gear—was sitting in the only dry corner in the warehouse. I took off my shoes, rolled up my pants, grabbed an extra mop, and joined the cleanup. After so much hospitality, I was glad for the opportunity to pitch in.

That afternoon I unpacked the shipment, cutting through all the duct tape and disgusting, greasy carpet. After a journey of thousands of miles, it still smelled like cat piss. But everything inside had survived well.

Meanwhile, people were tracking me down. The BBC was calling, Portuguese television channels wanted to arrange interviews, and the Associated Press correspondent in Lisbon was writing a story. Apparently, everyone had seen the piece in *Espresso.*

Everyone including the customs officials, who, Francisco informed me, were demanding a letter of apology. Although they didn't know how to categorize the boat for tax purposes, they resented my insinuation that they might hold us up. Francisco had already prepared the letter and told me, chortling, that Olga's strategy had worked. Caught in the spotlight, customs would probably release the boat quickly. That Olga, I thought, she'd do well in Washington.

There was other news, too. A gentleman representing a vintner by the name of JP Vinhos had also phoned. Where could he ship me, as a gift, some of their newest wine? I would be the first person outside the vineyard to try it, he said. And the reason for this generosity? I had mentioned their name in *Espresso,* and they were grateful for the publicity. I didn't tell him the truth—namely, that when the reporter had asked me what my favorite Portuguese wines were, I was too embarrassed to plead total ignorance. So I mentioned the only Portuguese wine I could remember trying, one that bore my own initials: JP.

At the end of the day, I called Garth. He was still having trouble with the sail, and would not be arriving as scheduled. Working almost around the clock, he had been vomiting from the stress. I felt terrible for him. The *Cork Boat,* while a lot of work, was supposed to be fun at least sometimes. Over here in

Portugal, it definitely was. But back in Mount Pleasant, things were apparently anything but.

"Stop working," I told him. "Just get on a plane. Bring the sail as is. Bring the rudder. We'll finish everything here. The boat gets out of customs tomorrow."

He said he'd do the best he could.

Despite promising words from customs, my scheduling concerns were mounting. The original launch date had already passed, and I still hadn't seen the boat yet, let alone gotten it rigged, ready, and up the river to Barca. That in itself would take several days.

But not everyone could afford to wait. My parents, my cousin Sally, and a family friend had already arrived in Lisbon, and were making their way north to Porto. They had all planned a weeklong stay in Portugal on my assurances that the launch would happen during that window of time. But as always, the boat project was behind schedule.

Whatever the obstacle, I just had to get that boat into the water while they were here. They had saved the very first corks. There was no way I could let the launch slip any further.

That night, I lay in bed as thunder boomed across the city and lightning slashed the sky. It was as dramatic a storm as I'd seen in years. I have always loved thunderstorms, and I took this one as a good omen. I needed things to break my way.

————

Not surprisingly, they didn't. The next day, after waiting until midafternoon for customs to process the requisite paperwork, I finally got the boat. Or, rather, I got permission to take the boat, if I could figure out a way to move it.

Secured inside a green, forty-foot steel shipping container, the boat appeared to be in good shape. It's just that the truck hired to move the boat was designed to carry diminutive European cars, not a twenty-two-foot cork boat. The truck did have a tilting, hydraulic bed as I had specified, but it was too short. At least a quarter of the boat would be dangling off the back, which could easily cause a catastrophic rupture. I asked if a bigger truck were available.

The answer was a disappointing no: a European Union regulation apparently prohibited bigger trucks of this type. To make matters worse, I had just insulted the driver by questioning the size of his vehicle.

"Let's just use two forklifts," he suggested, gruffly. "We'll just pick up your boat at either end and put it on the truck." A crew of young forklift operators, who had set aside their motorcycle magazines to join our deliberations, nodded in agreement. You could almost hear them revving their engines in anticipation.

"Yes, but even if the boat survives," I answered, "how would I get it off, at the other end?"

He shrugged, and took another drag on his cigarette.

My Portuguese was limited, but I knew the word for no.

The driver, fed up, got into his truck and drove off, his

wheels kicking up a cloud of dust. With all potential for excitement over, the forklift operators wandered off back to their study of the latest crotch rockets. I kicked a loose rock in frustration, and stared at my favorite headache, the *Cork Boat.*

As I pondered my options, a ferret-like man approached to warn me that the warehouse would be closing in half an hour. "It's not our job to move the boat," he reminded me, "only to provide the space."

I would have to come back the next day, with a new plan. The boat would be spending the night here, in its box. My eyes swept the dusty freight yard, its broken pallets, old tires, razor wire fencing, and sketchy surroundings. A vandal with a knife could make short work of the boat. "Do you have a padlock?" I asked the ferret. Just by chance, I had learned the word for padlock, *cadeado,* the day before.

He laughed, showing his teeth. A padlock would do nothing, he said. Not in this neighborhood. But he would have the container secured. He summoned one of his men, who fired up the biggest forklift I had ever seen—a forklift almost as big as my entire apartment. As casually as I might parallel park, the forklift operator picked up another forty-foot steel container from across the yard, swung it around, and slammed it against the door of my container with a violent, metallic boom. Setting it down and withdrawing his fork, he parked his machine, turned it off, and pocketed the ignition key. Nobody would get to the boat tonight—at least not without an acetylene torch or a crane.

Frustrated, I called Jorge. In Portugal, when all else failed, that was all I could do. I felt bad calling him all the time—he had clients to serve, and corks to sell—but I needed his help. I had lost a day I couldn't afford, and had to figure out a way to move the boat. He drove out to pick me up, and we drove into Porto to search out another truck.

A sympathetic garage owner listened to our problem, and dialed the cell phone of one of his drivers. Could he do a special job? The driver, who happened to be in his wrecker at the moment, wasn't interested. He was heading out to dinner with his wife and daughter. But when he heard the specifics of our plight, he agreed to meet us at a certain highway exit, so long as we could get there within fifteen minutes. Jorge looked at his watch. It was rush hour. We would need a little luck, but we could make it.

Twenty minutes later, we pulled up. My heart sank. The man's truck was the same model as the other one. From the cab, his daughter, clearly unhappy with us for postponing her dinner, stuck out her tongue. How did I come to be here, I wondered, chasing down tow trucks in suburban Portugal?

The driver, a nice enough fellow, listened politely as we apologized for having wasted his time. Though eager to get on to dinner, he assured us it was no trouble. But if we were interested, he added, he did know a fellow who drove an even bigger truck, EU regulations be damned.

"A bigger truck?" Jorge asked. "How big?"

"Go see for yourself. He's at an accident, maybe a kilometer up the road. I just passed him on my way over here, ten minutes ago."

Thanking him, we got back in the car. Jorge gunned it, back up onto the highway. Sure enough, just up the road were flashing lights. And there was the holy grail: the largest, most beautiful, hydraulic flatbed I had ever laid eyes on. It was a Mercedes, and even larger than Salah's truck back in Washington.

The police were waving all of us rubberneckers past, but I scribbled down the phone number from the truck's door. And with one quick call to its dispatcher, we had that truck scheduled for the morning.

When I got back to the hotel that evening, my parents had arrived, along with my cousin Sally, my friend Deb Nichols, and our family friend Joanie Binkow. When we had first gotten sponsorship for the Douro expedition, Garth and I had issued a blanket invitation to any and all friends and family to join us in Portugal. Only a few were able to get away on such short notice.

Sally, a figure painter who had just received her MFA from a prestigious British art school, had flown down from her home in London. She and I were extremely close, and always encouraged each other's creative endeavors. Working as a flight attendant for many years, she always had corks for me wherever we met, whether our rendezvous was in Omaha,

Paris, or Istanbul. Deb, a semiretired hedge-fund manager, whom I'd last seen that final hectic weekend of construction before the dry launch, had flown in from Chicago. Joanie, a successful entrepreneur in video post-production, also had the independence of spirit and schedule to travel as she pleased. And having given me her fair share of corks over the past couple of years, she certainly wasn't going to miss the launch for anything.

I was excited to see them all and took everybody, including Jorge, out for a celebratory dinner. Over the past week, my working relationship with Jorge had evolved into friendship. Bright, energetic, and charming, he took easily to my friends and family, and I was glad for the opportunity to include him in the festivities. At his suggestion, we ate at Chez Lapin, an elegant little restaurant tucked into an eighteenth-century stone archway on a street overlooking the Douro.

At anchor, just across the river, lay a dozen port boats, their decks stacked high with barrels. Beyond them, the lights of Vila Nova de Gaia twinkled in the night. In ten days or so, I told the group, the *Cork Boat* will be finishing its voyage right there.

My mom offered a toast. "To my son, for never giving up a child's dreams, while making them real with an adult's capacity."

A lump in my throat, I toasted my parents in return. I thanked them for saving corks for so many years, and for their enduring faith in me.

My dad offered the final words, and we all raised our glasses. "*O barco!* To the boat!"

The next morning, the big truck made short work of loading. Hooked to a winch, the boat rolled easily out of the container and up onto the truck. Relations with the driver went smoothly, too. Whereas yesterday's driver had been a testy *macho*, today's turned out to be a generous, spirited *fado* singer. Driving trucks was António's day job; singing Portugal's melancholic ballads was his passion. The boat spoke to that same human passion, he said.

Down at Global, an hour later, the boat rolled off and into the warehouse, just as easily as it had rolled on. There were four cases of wine and champagne waiting, from JP Vinhos. The note accompanying them read: "Congratulations for having the persistence to make such an amazing dream become real."

At midday, I picked Garth up from the airport in a Cork Supply truck. He was exhausted from jet lag and weeks of hard labor, but he was excited to finally arrive. I was pumped to see him, too. Not just on a practical level, but on a personal one. Despite our periodic conflicts, I loved his company. As a fellow from Cork Supply drove us back to Global, I gave Garth a quick briefing on where we stood—the people, the resources, the challenges, the schedule. We have a great workshop, lots of help, transportation lined up, and two and a half days to assemble the boat, I said. And we have lots of coffee— very good coffee, too.

When we unwrapped the rudder he had labored so hard to build, I could see it was a work of art. It was beautiful as well as functional. I now understood why it had taken days and days to design, build, sand, stain, and urethane. His perfectionism showed. The sail wasn't done, and the iron-on transfers didn't look so good, but we'd fix that. Besides, the whole boat looked a little homemade—a raggedy sail would suit it fine.

The next few days seemed to repeat so many past episodes in the *Cork Boat* saga—long hours of whining drills, rasping sandpaper, and hard physical labor. Once again, I grew well acquainted with a concrete floor, and had the joy of borrowing another set of car jacks to boost the boat up, section by section, as we finished attaching the decks. Thankfully, this time, Garth and I had a lot in the way of help.

Everybody around us was eager to pitch in. While the friendly staff at Global and Cork Supply hunted down tools and materials, my mom and Deb spent the better part of a day ironing the last of the transfers onto the sail. Sally, the artist, took up a paintbrush to waterproof the rudder and the last of our three decks. Joanie cut foam rubber for seat cushions and covered them in extra sailcloth. My dad, Garth, and Brandt, who had flown in that night, joined me in figuring out the boat's rigging. Others brought us food, and Olga managed the camera crews that kept coming in and out to film these crazy Americans in their final, hectic preparations.

By late Friday night, there were just three of us left: Garth,

Brandt, and myself. "Just two more hours" became our motto, as completion kept receding into the night, an hour at a time. "Just two more hours."

Our Portuguese workshop was much nicer than the Boat Works, and we were in a foreign country, listening to unintelligible DJs spin their tunes, but it all felt so familiar. How many "last nights" had there been on this boat? Three? Four? In my bleary state, I couldn't quite remember.

In a quiet moment, I took out my knife and cut a small slit in the netting at the stern of the boat. Somehow, in the crazy, final night of construction before our "dry" launch in Washington, a log was built one cork short. The resulting gap was hardly noticeable, and given the scale of the boat, a missing cork didn't matter one bit. But I had a special cork to fill it— one of Marlene's, from those she had saved for the boat. I wanted her with me on the trip.

Sometime around three A.M. we drove back to Porto and fell into bed for a few hours of sleep. In the morning, the *Cork Boat* would be heading up to Barca de Alva.

Onto the Douro

W̶e set off late, about noon, but at least the boat was done and on the road. Our anticipation was mounting. Not that we knew what to expect. Nobody in our party knew anything about Barca de Alva, really, except that it was a small village near the Spanish border. Garth and I had picked it as a starting point for that sole geographic reason. We thought it would be cool to cross the entire country, from Spain to the sea.

None of the Portuguese we had talked to knew anything about Barca, either. Jorge's wife, Zé, told me it was the *"cu de Judas"*—the ass of Judas—Portuguese slang for the middle of nowhere. Even António, our singing truck driver, had to search his map to find it. It turned out that there was no direct way there.

Most of our support crew—my parents, Deb, and Joanie—took the scenic route, which more or less followed the river. Jorge and Zé said they would find their own way, and meet us there at the end of the day. Other friends, who were flying in from England and renting a car, were on their own.

The rest of us formed a small convoy: António's truck, a rental car, and a Jeep Cherokee driven by an Associated Press photographer named Paulo. Our route looked longer on the map, but António said the roads would be better, and easier on the boat.

We hadn't gone ten miles before a motorcycle cop spotted the truck and pulled it over. Following behind, we all pulled over, too. The scenario was all too familiar, only this time, with limited language skills, I would be working at a distinct disadvantage.

I got out of the Jeep and walked up to talk with the officer, who was asking António for the truck's papers. He was wearing black jackboots, and I could see the butt of a pistol jutting from his white leather holster. His whole get-up smacked of fascism and I tried, unsuccessfully, to remember just exactly when military rule had ended in Portugal.

"*Boa tarde!*" I offered, in my best Portuguese—my language skills had been improving lately. "*Que tal?*" How's it going?

He wasn't impressed.

"*É um barco de rolhas,*" I tried again, "*sem nenhuma gota da cola.*" It's a cork boat, without a drop of glue. "*Vamos a—*"

He cut off my efforts, dismissively. "I know, I know," he interrupted. "I listened to you explain it all this morning, on TV."

I shut up. The truck's papers, fortunately, were in order. He waved us on.

The drive to Barca de Alva, across dry hills that rose to mountains, first on a major highway and then on narrow, winding roads, took all afternoon. As the sun dropped low in the sky, we found ourselves inching our vehicles through flocks of bleating sheep, their bells clanking as they crossed the road to another pasture. Villagers stared as the truck passed, no doubt wondering about the enormous object strapped to its bed.

We pulled into Barca just before dusk. Our entire crew was waiting for us at an outdoor café, cold bottles of beer already in hand. The village could not have been more perfect: crumbling stone houses with small iron balconies overlooking a few cobbled streets; an old, rusting bridge, its slanting trusses black against the setting sun; and a snug, modest waterfront, where a few boats, their mooring lines slack, floated serenely in the fading light. I could hardly believe it—we were finally here!

I wanted nothing more than to join the others, pop open a beer, and savor the moment. But there wasn't time. António was heading back to Porto that night; we would have to unload the boat immediately and get it into the water before we lost the last of our daylight.

Within minutes, everybody was pitching in, unloading everything that had been strapped flat on the boat. Then

António backed the truck down the village boat ramp, tilted the flatbed, and slowly unwound the winch.

Wearing jeans still grimy from days of labor back at the warehouse, I waded waist-deep into the water, guiding the boat in. I felt for all the world like General MacArthur, striding through the surf in the Philippines after having promised, years earlier, "I shall return." Years earlier I had made a similar promise to myself. I would build a cork boat. And here it was, finally afloat in the Douro.

Garth and I high-fived, hard. And then, knives in hand, we quickly cut through the taut webbing that strapped the dollies to the boat, and pulled them out from underneath. It felt great to be cutting them loose. The boat had never before floated without those damned training wheels. At the first launch, in the Potomac, we had been too worried about getting them back on again. But this was no test. This time we were going all the way down the river, to Porto. Through every bend and every dam, 133 miles, until we crossed under the soaring steel trusses of Porto's signature bridge, a span designed by a protégé of the great Eiffel himself.

The crowd—and there was a crowd now—started clapping. Climbing aboard, Garth and I rowed the boat over to the nearby dock, where people helped us tie up. An aging fisherman in a small wooden boat, his stout wife standing in the bow, motored up to the next slip. They had come to take a closer look.

"It's a beautiful boat," he said.

"Will it make it to Porto?" someone asked him.

"Eh," he said, nodding. "The boat, yes. The boys, I don't know . . ."

Everybody laughed.

We stayed that night at the only hotel in town. Our party took all six rooms. Its small lobby became our staging area, strewn with life jackets, dry bags, miscellaneous tools, extra sailcloth, spools of line, spare netting, and rolls of duct tape. We laid our four long oars and our sixteen-foot mast in the only place they would fit, on the floor of the hotel's kitchen, just in front of the wood-burning stove.

And from that stove came a feast. It was hearty fare—steak, potatoes, and crusty loaves of bread—laid at a long table seating twenty. I sat at one end and Garth at the other, the two of us truly amazed that our boat was finally in the water, that such a crew had gathered to celebrate, and that we were about to embark on this most unlikely of journeys.

Words, like the local wine, flowed freely. Jorge spoke of "a dream in the shape of a cork boat." I toasted Garth as "a brilliant designer and a partner as stubborn as I am," and thanked him for pouring his creativity and determination into seeing the project through. He toasted me in turn, wondering aloud how I had managed to corral so many people into helping us. "I don't know how you did it," he said, "but you did." It was an honest, tearful, generous exchange, one in which, perhaps for the first time, we fully acknowledged our debt to, and our admiration for, one another.

Then António stood to clear his throat, and the table fell silent. And this *fadista*, who drove a truck to earn his daily bread, who had skipped his own radio show to see a boat made of corks into the river he loved, started to sing. Many of the words of his melancholic ballad were lost on me, but the music was not. It struck a chord in me, touching notes both of loss and of hope. When he finished, I rose to thank him and all the others who had made the journey possible, and to say why, in the face of loss, hope and celebration were so important.

Tears flowing, I spoke of saving corks, in the beginning with my sister, Sara, for a boat she never got to see, and how I saved them over a lifetime she never got to live. I spoke of my parents, who had endured such terrible loss yet still managed to celebrate life's finest moments with joy. That had been a lesson for me. "The hard knocks are inevitable," I said. "The good times, the dreams, those you have to reach for. And I want to thank all of you, and all of those people who couldn't be here tonight, for making my dream possible."

Around the table people were dabbing away tears. Not, I understood, for my losses, but for their own. This moment wasn't really about the *Cork Boat* anymore. It was about their own hopes and dreams, their own sadness, and their own joy.

As midnight approached, people pushed back from the

table. We were all exhausted and, with a big day ahead, needed sleep badly. But later, lying in bed, I found I was unable to let go of the evening just yet. It had been too perfect, one in which I felt briefly transcendent, just as I had that night in New York when Marlene played in Tamar's show and I realized that life *could* be absolutely perfect, if only for a few moments at a time.

All was quiet now, save for a soft night breeze rustling the leaves of the tree beside my balcony, and the murmur of two old men at the outdoor café across the street, talking into the night. Trying to imagine the voyage ahead, I finally drifted off.

The beeping alarm on my watch woke me at seven, and it took me a long moment to realize where I was. Excited but still a little bleary-eyed, I pulled on some clothes and made my way down to the dock to check on the boat. It was just fine, except for one thing: an eighty-foot ghost ship, rusting and apparently abandoned, had drifted downstream over-night, and was blocking the boat in its slip. This ship, its wheelhouse windows missing and a broken crane rising from its deck, must have been dragging anchor when we arrived the night before.

"We don't know where it came from," a man explained. "It just drifted in."

Just drifted in? Here was a ship that had clearly been on the river many years. It was trapped between one dam at the

Spanish border, and another dam twenty miles downstream. I could even make out its name on the rusting bow, *Duriense.* How could the townsfolk not know where it came from? And why had the winds and the currents conspired to put it, at this moment in its dwindling life afloat, in the one spot on the entire Douro River where it could block our boat in its slip?

Somehow, we'd have to move this behemoth before we could depart. At the moment, I just added a mental note— "move ship"—to the morning's growing to-do list.

Seeing me up and about, a few sleepy camera crews approached. They had gotten up even earlier than I had to film the boat's departure. *"Desculpe,"* I said, apologizing. "We are late." I told them we would not be launching as scheduled, at seven-thirty. "Go get some coffee," I urged. "You won't miss anything."

They groaned, none too happy to have risen at the crack of dawn on a Sunday morning—in *"cu de Judas,"* no less—to shoot B-roll footage of a cork boat that was now running several hours behind schedule. Promising them a full press conference before we shoved off, I went off in search of some coffee myself.

Over the course of the morning, as we rigged the boat and loaded it with gear, food, and water, a small crowd gathered on the quay. The widows in black seemed particularly interested; I hoped it wasn't an omen.

Although a few of the local kids had questions about the boat, most people already knew the basics. Apparently, there had been a story about our project in the local paper a few days earlier. Barca de Alva hadn't seen such a commotion, we were told, since the railroad tracks were ripped up a decade earlier.

As we stepped the mast and pulled the rigging taut, the Stars and Stripes fluttered proudly from one backstay, a Portuguese ensign from the other. For diplomacy's sake, we placed both flags at the same height. Given the U.S. soccer team's recent upset of Portugal in the World Cup, it seemed especially prudent. At the top of the mast we flew the pennant of the University of Michigan: a yellow block M on a blue field. Whatever our differences, Garth and I would always be united in our die-hard passion for the Wolverines. The flapping flags looked great together. The cameras whirred and clicked.

Finally, we were ready. After a brief press conference, a few photos on the boat, and a long hug from my parents, Garth and I took our positions at the oars. The ghost ship *Duriense* had drifted several feet upstream again, but its stern was still jutting past our slip; could we squeeze past it into open water? We couldn't risk it; its jagged, rusting rudder might slice our boat to ribbons. That hulk would have to move.

In an instant, a half-dozen men and boys had grabbed the cables that trailed from the ship. On the count of three, they leaned into their traces. For a long moment, nothing happened. If the *Cork Boat* weighed over a ton, then that rusting hulk must have weighed that a hundred times over. But then, to the grunts of those pulling, and ever so slowly, the *Duriense* began to surrender its position.

Seizing the moment, we shoved off into the river. People clapped and cheered. The *Cork Boat* was free and clear.

On Garth's stroke, we began to row. A hundred yards downriver, I hoisted the sail. It caught the breeze and billowed out with a soft thump. Moving smartly under sail now, we stowed oars, and watched the people waving on shore recede into the distance.

Perhaps it was just as well that I didn't hear the remark that an old villager, on watching us depart, made to Joanie: "I've been on this river a long time, and it's not as easy as it looks." In any case, I don't think his warning would have changed our plans. We were taking the *Cork Boat* all the way to Porto, no matter what.

A few minutes later, the press boat—a fisherman's dory with an outboard that had been puttering around us with a handful of photographers—headed back upriver. And then, rounding a bend, Garth and I found ourselves suddenly alone, sailing down the Douro.

As Garth settled into the bow for a nap, I took the tiller and steered us downriver. It felt fantastic—and a little surreal—to finally be off and away. The boat was finished, the hubbub was behind us, and the journey stretched ahead. The peacefulness of the river was absolutely wonderful.

I surveyed our surroundings. The hills that rose on either side of us were dry and rocky, covered mostly with scrub and the occasional olive tree. Sometime in the distant past these hills had been vineyards. Their slopes were still ribbed here and there with crumbling stone terraces that climbed upward, step by step, to the blue sky. This was the sort of landscape I had always imagined.

Our first rendezvous point was a place called Almendra, several miles downriver. It was the first spot the road dipped down to the water, and our crew, who had generously offered to pack up the gear we'd left strewn in the hotel lobby, said they'd meet us there. Maybe we'd pick up our first passenger there for the cruise to the dam at Pocinho.

The Pocinho dam, about twenty miles from Barca de Alva, was our day's final destination. It was an ambitious goal, especially since we had gotten off to a late start. But the wind was steady, and we still had eight hours of daylight. We had notified the Dam Authority of our expected arrival time and wanted to be in position to go through the lock as scheduled, first thing the following morning. If we had to push today, so be it. We could take it easy tomorrow.

About an hour out of Barca de Alva, though, the wind suddenly shifted against us. In a normal sailboat, sailing upwind is no problem at all. In fact, tacking into the wind is practically the first lesson you learn in a sailing course. It's a standard maneuver.

But we weren't in a standard sailboat. We were in a two-thousand-pound boat made of wine corks and rubber bands, and flying a square sail of limited size. We had sacrificed our capacity for upwind sailing on the altar of aesthetics. After all, we were floating down a river. The current would carry us— or so the theory went.

I dropped the sail.

"We'd better start rowing," Garth said, rousing himself from the bow.

Ah, rowing! It sounded romantic. What was a little workout, anyway? Just a way to get tan and buff at the same time, and arrive in Porto a bronzed god. Taking our places at the oars, we started to row. It felt good. At least, it did for the first five or ten minutes.

The wind, unfortunately, was still rising against us. But what could we do about it? Nothing. We kept rowing. As a distraction, I started measuring our progress against landmarks on shore. Off to port was an old stone house, long abandoned, its door ajar and its red-tiled roof sagging with age.

"Check out that house, Garth!" I said.

I wondered who had lived there, and why they had left. I had read that in the nineteenth century, the vineyards of the Douro valley had been devastated by a root disease that killed off thousands of vines and sent an entire generation of Portuguese in search of work in coastal cities, even abroad. Many never returned.

But as I rowed along, admiring the house, I realized that something was slightly amiss: the house wasn't moving. It was still there off to port despite our efforts to move downriver. And the wind had started kicking up small whitecaps.

We started pulling harder. I thought back to Valdemar's warning, a week earlier, when I had visited Pinhão. In his wooden launch, with its big, black sixty-horse Mercury outboard, the river's headwinds had seemed just another potential worry. Now they were an actual problem.

"Check out that house, Garth," I said, making a flat attempt at humor. It was still off to port. Every four or five strokes, one of our oars would slip, then jam in its oarlock. We hadn't yet mounted the special braces, called oar-rights, that Garth had purchased to prevent this problem. They were stowed in our gear, ashore. All we could do was curse, jerk the offending oar loose, and keep on rowing.

Finally, about four o'clock, the wind died, and we took a break. The respite gave us a chance to unroll our charts, a series of oversized Douro valley topographic maps that we kept in a map tube lashed to the base of the mast. My dad, who loves all things cartographic, had found them in the map library at the University of Michigan and had photocopied a set for our trip. There were ten of them, each covering a section of the river, all the way to Porto.

Drifting at a virtual standstill, we took a reading from our handheld GPS unit. In three hours, it looked like we had only covered about three miles. Reaching the dam at Pocinho today was out of the question. We'd have to settle for the rendezvous at Almendra.

In the stifling heat of late afternoon, the water was perfectly still, a blinding mirror broken only by the perpetual dip, pull, and return of our oars and the occasional jumping fish. Now I understood what Pedro Negrão had meant when he said his riverboat captains think of the Douro "as a series of large lagoons." With all the dams closed, there just wasn't any current.

Any thoughts of a leisurely float through wine country had to be thrown overboard. Hell, it could take a month to get to Porto at this rate.

Two hours later, a little light-headed from the sun, we rounded a bend to see a row of wooden fishing boats and a small sandy beach just ahead, off to port. Then we saw our crew, just up the beach. They spotted us, too, and the chant went up, across the glassy water: *"Cork Boat! Cork Boat! Cork Boat!"*

Almendra. Five hours of hard rowing. Five miles by river. We could have walked there faster. Our centerboard, which had jammed in the down position, ground into the sand a few yards off the bank. We waded ashore.

Our crew was in good cheer. After the launch, they had packed up our extra gear, eaten lunch, and spent the next few hours exploring the countryside. The women even went skinny-dipping in the river. They were all upbeat and energetic, but Garth and I were totally beat. Schedule or no schedule, dam or no dam, there was no way we could go any farther that day.

Almendra, it turned out, was an abandoned railway station at the terminus of a potholed, dead-end spur off the highway. The depot itself was a shell, but still boasted pretty blue *azulejos* and railings of curled wrought iron. Even though it felt like the middle of nowhere, my dad said we really weren't that far from civilization. The nearest town was only half an hour's drive away.

Great, but what to do with the boat? Neither Garth nor I wanted to camp out, not if we were going to get up and row again in the morning. We decided that we'd just have to leave it unguarded overnight. If the handful of sunbathers on the beach were vandals, so be it.

So Garth tied the boat's painter—the line off our bow—securely to a tree and we all hiked up through the brush to the road. As we piled into the cars, I cast a last look over my shoulder, but couldn't see the boat—only the very top of its mast and the yellow M on our pennant, stirring ever so slightly. Then we drove up into the hills, leaving the river behind.

That night we stayed in a *residencial,* a small hotel, in the nearest town, a prosperous agricultural center called Vila Nova de Foz Côa. Translated, the name means "new town at the mouth of the Côa." The Côa was a small tributary of the Douro.

It was a pleasant community of well-kept houses and narrow, cobbled streets that were lined with small shops. We brought the maps to dinner and, beers in hand, held a navigation powwow. The irony of so many beer drinkers on a cork boat was not lost on anyone, but after a hard, hot day on the river, a cold beer really hit the spot. It had been that way during construction, too. I had heard there was a Belgian brewery that sealed its bottles with corks, and had hoped to use one in the boat, but I never came across their beer.

Our "map meeting" over dinner that night was the start of what would become, over the course of the journey, an extremely productive, collaborative decision-making process. How far had we come? How far did we want to go—or, rather, how far could we get? Was there a town or a village, or even a road intercept, where we could stop to seek lodging for the night?

Although our maps showed that riverside towns and villages would become much more frequent the closer we got to Porto, the upper reaches of the Portuguese Douro were largely unpopulated, flanked by relative wilderness or expansive, terraced *quintas*. We had not come equipped to camp out, and had no desire to, either. And while we didn't need luxury, we sure looked forward to ending each day with a hot shower, a decent meal, and a real bed.

Given our first day's progress, it didn't look like we would make the dam for another two days. We would probably have to spend a few more nights in Foz Côa as we rowed west.

By cell phone I checked in with Jorge at Cork Supply,

and with Olga, who reported that our launch was all over the national news. Reporters had been calling her all day for updates; a few wanted to join us on the river for part of the journey.

"Listen," I said. "The boat is great, but this trip is going to take a *lot* longer than we had planned. It was really hard going, and we only made eight kilometers. I have no idea when we're going to get into Porto."

"That's fine," Olga said, laughing. "I will tell them the journey is very difficult and that you are rowing hard." She knew, as I did, that dealing with the press depends, in large part, on managing expectations. The fact that we were having difficulties—that the river was teaching us a thing or two— only made for a better story. The press was invested in our voyage now, and our struggles would only whet their appetite for more.

But as pleased as I was about the media interest (vestiges of my Washington instincts, perhaps), it seemed now a distant abstraction. Beyond the banks of the river, beyond the wind and the sun and the dams and the places we might stay, beyond the intimate confines of our little vessel and its immediate surroundings, the world had begun to fade away. We might have been casual or presumptuous in tackling the Douro, but we had thrown down a glove, and the river was answering our challenge. It would have us on its own terms, it seemed, whether we were in a hurry or not.

And I realized something now about those *azulejos* at the

Douro Azul office—the ones depicting oxen hauling the *barcos rabelos* from towpaths on the banks. They were pulling those old port boats *downstream,* into the westerly winds. Now we had become those oxen, beasts of our own burden, and the river would demand no less from us. We were in the yoke, and it was going to be a long, sweaty pull to Porto.

But my blood was up for the challenge, and I knew Garth's was, too. He loved tough physical challenges, even more than I did, especially those pitting him against the elements.

Once, on a twenty-four-hour exploration of South Dakota's Jewel Cave, the passageway Garth and his companions were traversing got narrower and narrower. Soon he was crawling on his hands and knees, then on his belly, for hundreds of slow, agonizing yards. "It was like being under your bed," he said, "with sharp stones cutting through your clothes."

After many hours in the cave, they ran out of water. They now faced the prospect of dehydration, and the very real possibility of total darkness; the fuel pellets in their carbide headlamps depended on a chemical reaction with water to produce the gas they burned for light. Their only choice was to urinate into their headlamps, which then provided light, but also kept dribbling down their faces for seven interminable, parched hours of crawling. "You just couldn't freak out," Garth said. "It wasn't an option."

No, I wouldn't have to worry about Garth. He was as tough as they came.

A HARD ROW

Tough as Garth was, he was also—when it came to the outdoors, at least—a realist. We both agreed that since it looked like we were going to have to row all the way to Porto, we needed more people at the oars. Although Garth had designed the boat's deck system for two rowers, one sitting in front of the other, our craft was wide enough to accommodate two abreast, for a total of four rowers. So the next morning we took my parents aboard and put them to work.

Originally, they had been scheduled to fly home a few days earlier, but despite my dad's aggravation with the price-gougers at the airline, he had paid for their flight so they could celebrate the boat's belated launch in Barca de Alva and spend a little time on the river. After all, they hadn't spent three decades saving corks for the boat only to miss out on its maiden voyage altogether. I was thrilled they had decided to stay.

As we rowed through the morning, the landscape became greener and more cultivated, until it appeared that every square foot of hillside was terraced for viticulture. I had read that the Romans first terraced these hillsides two thousand years ago, coaxing hardy vines from the slate soil to help slake the thirst of their empire. They were so successful, in fact, that during the first century A.D., the emperor Domitian had ordered half the vineyards on the Iberian peninsula destroyed, to drive up prices. Now the European Union was limiting production all over Europe for similar reasons. So what had really changed in two thousand years?

From our perspective, not all that much. Except for the drone of an occasional pump, or the cloud of dust rising behind a distant tractor on a faraway terrace, we could easily have been galley slaves, rowing laboriously toward the Roman seaport of Portucale.

Watching my parents row, I was proud. My mom was almost sixty, and my dad sixty-five, but they seemed to be faring well. Both had grown up around boats; my mom in northern Michigan, and my dad on fishing and canoe trips in the Boundary Waters of Minnesota and Canada.

My dad had even built his own pontoon boat in college, on New York's Lake Cayuga. He had come across the original license for that boat while I was building the *Cork Boat,* and had sent me a photocopy. Under MAKE OF VESSEL he had typed: "Original Design." For inspiration, I had taped that license, circa 1958, to my refrigerator, along with the yellow Post-it note he had affixed. "There's a story to this," he had written. "Boat-building must be in the genes."

The next morning we got up before dawn and walked from our *residencial* to the little bakery in Foz Côa, where we had stayed a second night because we couldn't row far enough to warrant moving camp downstream. Tired and sore and still short of our first day's goal—the dam at Pocinho—we nursed our espressos, reluctant to pull ourselves away from the bakery's deliciously warm, chocolate-scented air. We were determined to make the dam today and had notified the Dam Authority that we would arrive by noon. Really, we said. This time we mean it. We had another motive for hitting the dam at lunchtime, too. Just below the dam, the river took a sharp turn to the north. If we traveled that stretch in the early afternoon, the prevailing winds, usually our enemy, might help push us along. Who knew how far we might get?

We were bringing aboard fresh rowers, too, subbing my parents out for Brandt, Deb, and Joanie, who happened to be celebrating her sixtieth birthday. Having traveled as shore crew for two days, they were all gung-ho to take their turns at the oars.

When my dad dropped us off at the Foz Côa railroad bridge, the boat was just as we had left it, tied securely to the rusting trestles. Within ten minutes, everything was stowed, and our new crew was pulling smoothly through the morning waters. Having five people aboard enabled us to put four at the oars, and one at the tiller. With someone to steer now and half the crew fresh, we made good time. Such good time, in fact, that we pulled up to the dock just above the dam at ten-thirty, a full hour and a half ahead of schedule. We had covered five miles in a single morning. It was a new record. If it had taken us three days instead of one to reach the dam, so what? We had the system down now.

Or so we thought. At noon, having scouted out potential landing sites downstream, we were back on board, pulling confidently for the lock, just across the river. We had all donned life jackets for the passage, which sounded pretty straightforward. The lockmaster would open the first sluice-gate, we would row into the lock, and the sluice-gate would close behind us. The lockmaster would then open valves to drain most of the water inside the lock, dropping us slowly until we were floating at the same level as the water below the dam. Finally, he would open the second sluice-gate and we would row out, on down the river.

Still, we weren't sure what to expect. It was a big dam—more than half a football field high. And we had never done this before. The only other time I had passed through a lock was when I was eight or nine years old, on a boat tour through the Soo locks in Michigan's Upper Peninsula, and I wasn't sure that experience really counted.

Rowing into position before the big gate, we could see that a few dozen people had gathered on the observation platform above. Among them, I spotted Senhor Carneiro, the wizened, tippling proprietor of our *residencial* in Foz Côa. He smiled and waved; he had driven over to see our boat. We waved back.

After what seemed an interminable wait, a bell rang, and the lock's enormous steel gate started rumbling into action, slowly dropping into the water in a churning hiss of bubbles. And then the wind hit us, hard.

"Row!" Deb yelled. She was at the tiller, looking ahead. The rest of us were at the oars, facing astern, and we started pulling hard. If the first day's rowing had been surprisingly difficult, this was demanding everything we had.

Apparently, the afternoon wind, roaring up the broad valley below the dam, was being channeled through the lock's narrow concrete walls, forming a wind tunnel. And we were rowing—or trying to row—straight into it.

"Row!" Deb yelled again as we kept pulling. The wind dropped for a moment, and we surged forward. "Here comes the wind again!" Deb yelled, her voice now a booming echo off the concrete walls. "Here comes the wind!"

I glanced over my shoulder, quickly, to see the telltale froth of whitecaps skipping across the water, just before the gust hit. This time it caught our bow, and spun us nearly sideways.

"Look out for the wall!" Deb shouted. "We're going to hit!"

It was too late. We tried to pull in our portside oars, but we weren't fast enough. They crunched into the wall and we lost our capacity to steer. All we could do was shove off again, clumsily, to be blown backward and out of the lock. The dam had just spit us out, as if we were a cherry pit.

"Everyone listen up," Garth said. "Let's line it up again. We'll go on Deb's command. Everybody listen to Deb. And stay calm."

We tugged our life jackets a little tighter, and once again, on Deb's command, rowed hard into the lock. Again the wind hit, but we struggled forward. We were aiming for a pylon on one wall, and as we drew close I yanked my oar in and scrambled for the bow, trying to loop the pylon with a line to pull us in. My toss fell short, just before the wind shoved us, with a crunch of oars, into the concrete wall to starboard.

This time, the wind turned us all the way around. We didn't fight it, and just let it push us back out, upriver. For the onlookers, it was probably entertaining. For my mom, high above us with the video camera, it was great footage. For us, it was humiliating. The dam operator, watching from his control tower above the lock, probably thought we were complete incompetents. First it had taken us three days to arrive instead of one, and now it would take us a third try, at least, just to get our boat into the lock, let alone out the other side. In my mind, I could just hear him calling up his buddies downstream, warning them about this hilarious rescue just waiting to happen.

But what could we do? We lined up again, with a new plan of attack. This time we would hit the wind harder than ever, straight up the gut. We would row past the pylon, then make a sharp turn to starboard, and drift back to it, sideways, with the wind. This way, our oars, which had survived their encounter with the wall, wouldn't get in the way, and Garth, the climber and rope king, would make the critical toss.

On Deb's command, we started rowing with renewed determination, straight into the wind's angry maw. Off whipped Brandt's baseball cap, into the drink. Then Garth's oar slipped, knocking Joanie hard in the back, and almost off her deck. But through it all we kept on pulling, leaning back into every stroke with all our weight. "Pull!" Deb yelled. "Pull!" Slowly, we made headway. And at just the right moment Deb shoved the tiller over to bring the boat around. Garth scrambled for the bow. His toss was good, and we were secure.

I looked up at the control tower to see the lockmaster leaning out, checking on us. I gave him a thumbs-up. His head disappeared. The sluice-gate behind us rumbled to life again, rising from the frothing waters, then clanged shut. We were in.

"Look out, Garth!" Brandt yelled. "It's moving!" The steel bollard to which we were temporarily moored—and which Garth had been leaning against—was dropping. Garth jumped back as we all suddenly realized how the system worked. Of course the bollard had to move, to correspond with the changing water level! That's why it rode on a motorized track, set into the wall, driven by something that looked like a giant bicycle chain.

The water began to drop fairly quickly, steadily exposing

taller and taller concrete walls, covered in black slime. As we dropped, all of us were a little awestruck by our surroundings. Behind us, the towering steel sluice-gate that held back an entire river groaned and squealed ominously, as water spouted from leaks and fell to the surface below. It was as if we had entered some industrial cathedral, its mechanical chorus asserting man's dominance over wind and waters, its engineers—not Mother Nature—granting us safe passage on our pilgrimage to the sea.

Soon enough, we were at the bottom, a tiny boat in a giant concrete chasm. The walls loomed above us, and the faces of those leaning over the railing looked like tiny gargoyles high overhead. As the sluice-gates ahead rumbled into motion, we steeled ourselves for the wind.

But as the gates swung open, we saw something much worse: a big Douro Azul riverboat, the biggest in their fleet. Engines churning, it looked like it was heading straight toward the lock—and us. A warning blast from its horn echoed off the dam, and although our reaction wasn't panic, it wasn't exactly pretty, either. With Garth and me yelling orders to Deb, who was still at the tiller, we all started pulling hard, oblivious to any wind that might have been blowing. Within thirty seconds or so, we managed to clear the oncoming disaster.

And then, as the barreling riverboat came abreast, we heard people cheering. Not just a few people cheering, but hundreds. Suddenly, it seemed, virtually everyone on the riverboat had come to the railing—the passengers with their flashing cameras, the ship's officers in their visored caps and gold braid, the bartenders in their black vests, even the cooks in their kitchen whites and tall hats. On three decks, at every open window and from every hatch, they were waving, cheering, and applauding, many with their hands over their heads.

Stunned but grinning, we waved back.

This unexpected salute, after three hard days on the river and a rough passage through the first dam, felt gratifying, exhilarating, and humbling all at once. We had needed a boost more than we knew.

As if to reward us for our journey's travails, the river veered north and our foe the wind shifted in our favor. Eagerly, I hoisted our sail and it whumped out, full in an instant. Within moments, the boat was racing downstream at such a clip that we started trailing a sizable wake. Exhausted from our somewhat chaotic passage through the dam, everybody stowed oars and relaxed. Topsheets in hand, I took the tiller, feeling like an ancient Greek charioteer. We were flying downriver now, and it felt absolutely glorious.

That night, we all went out for a farewell feast. My parents, Deb, and Joanie were due to leave in the morning for the long drive back to Lisbon and their flights home. Although the day had been our best yet, I was exhausted and worried about finding rowers for the next day. I had put in a call to the ever-optimistic Jorge, who said he would talk to some friends about driving out to help us row. But it was now past nine at night, and it looked like Garth, Brandt, and I would be continuing the voyage alone. Brandt, like Garth, was a warrior when it came to hard physical labor, but even so, we would be hard pressed as a trio.

As I scraped the last of the leftovers from empty platters, my mom leaned over and whispered, "I wish I could stay, but I have to get home." She had meetings scheduled with major donors to her organization, and couldn't stay. "But your father," she continued, "you should work on him. There's no reason he can't stay with the boat. I think you should encourage him to change his flight and go all the way down the river."

My mood brightened. I hadn't thought of that. On paper it made sense. He was a professor; it was summer; and his students were away. Sure, he had research under way, and administrative responsibilities, but it wasn't as if he had any classes to teach.

In reality, though, I knew it would be a tough sell. My dad was a practical guy. He tended to make decisions with his mind, not his heart. The first four-hundred-dollar change penalty, when he and my mom postponed their original return flight to stay for the launch, had almost sent him into orbit. It wasn't the money, I knew, it was the principle. But there was just no way he'd bend over the airline barrel a second time. Still, it couldn't hurt to try.

"H," I said, turning to him, "I know LP has to get back, but you should really think about staying. In addition to your good company, we could use your muscle. We don't have enough people to row. Why don't you stay on the boat with us and go all the way to Porto?"

Garth jumped into the fray right away. "Yeah. Come on, Hank. You're the navigator. We need you," he said.

And before my dad could answer, the whole table was noisily urging him to change his flight, stay on the boat, and continue on down the river.

"But I don't have any gear," he protested. "I don't have the—"

"Between the rest of us, we can hook you up with everything you need," insisted Garth.

I knew he was flattered, but was he starting to waver? Suddenly sensing real possibility, I turned up the heat. "Come on, H. You and me. Father and son. Down the river. All the way to Porto on the world's first cork boat!"

That was it. A big, mischievous grin spread across his face, as if he knew it was the boy in him, not the sixty-five-year-old professor, making the decision.

"Oh, what the hell! I'm staying!"

The table cheered.

After dinner, Jorge called. He had two friends willing to make the three-hour drive to meet up with us; their names were Matos and Lily, and they would arrive at our *residencial* sometime in the wee hours.

It was a short night of sleep for all of us. At six-thirty the original crew met for a last breakfast together, down at the bakery, where we could linger over our goodbyes. Joanie and Deb had had a great time. Greater, they both said, than they could have imagined.

"It's been the best trip of my life," Deb said. "You Pollacks have opened up a whole new world. I didn't know you could travel this way." Not by cork boat, she meant, but on the cheap, improvisationally, and off the beaten track. For her, roughing it had always meant making reservations at a four-star hotel instead of a five. Now she was crashing in *residenciales* for twelve bucks a night and skinny-dipping in the Douro.

Leaving the bakery, it was really hard to say goodbye to my mom. She had been the boat's biggest supporter—and mine— from the very beginning. If not for her encouragement, I might have dropped the entire project. I reminded her of her critical advice: "You're an organizer. Organize it," she had said. And so I had.

Inspired by my dad's decision to stay, she said she would try to return to Portugal before we arrived in Porto. "I don't want to miss the party!" she said.

OF DAMS AND DAMSELS

The gorge we tackled the next day made the wind back at the Pocinho dam seem almost easy. Discouraged after a long, fierce morning at the oars, we sought shelter in a small, jagged cove, hard beneath the towering cliffs.

We faced a tough choice: to push forward through the gorge in hopes that the wind would ease when the valley widened, or to turn back. With six of us aboard to take turns rowing, we decided to keep going. But two hours later, with the wind still pummeling us and the sun dropping low in the sky, Garth and I concluded there was no way to reach the next village before nightfall.

Reluctantly, we turned the boat back upriver and hoisted sail for the easy run back to our day's starting point, a little town called Foz do Sabor. As we raced upriver, the wind at our backs, I knew we had made the right decision. Still, it was a bitter one. If we had failed to muscle our way through this stretch of river with two extra crew members, how in hell were we going to make it downriver tomorrow, with only four of us? Were we doomed to a Sisyphean purgatory of row and return, row and return, never to reach Porto? Perhaps, unless we accepted a tow.

The prospect of accepting motorized assistance was anathema to me. It seemed somehow inelegant, like using glue to attach corks. It felt impure, as if we would be breaking the rules. But what rules? Was there some absolute moral imperative that stated: Thou shalt row the *Cork Boat* downstream no matter what? And who was setting "rules" for the *Cork Boat,* anyway? Just what was I trying to prove? I was a purist, yes. But I was also a realist. There were no rules governing the *Cork Boat* except those we set ourselves. We would look for a tow.

It was dusk when we finally tied up back at the dock in Foz do Sabor, and we found the local fishermen up at the village café putting down a few tumblers of the local port. As Matos explained our predicament, they nodded gravely and conferred in low voices. I had seen their boats, which were mostly clinker-built of rough-hewn planks, and powered by small outboards. They were beautiful, rustic craft, perfect for slow trolling the still, glassy waters of dawn. But pulling a one-ton cork boat, four extra men, and all their gear through the windiest gorge on the upper Douro?

Anything for a price, I learned. A tow the following day would cost us 225 euros (about $225). Although that wasn't a bank-breaker in the grand scheme of things, we were being taken for a ride, and we knew it. Given our ambivalence about tows in the first place, it felt like salt in the wound. But what choice did we have? We agreed to be ready in the morning. After taking Matos and Lily to dinner, we saw them off on their drive back to Porto, and turned in for the night. It had been an exhausting day, and we had gotten nowhere.

The sun was arcing toward noon, and we were still lolling about at the dock waiting for our tow to show up, when we realized it was the Fourth of July. With the Stars and Stripes fluttering from one of our backstays, we celebrated by singing a few patriotic songs.

Just as we were finishing, a white minibus appeared over the hill, heading toward the dock. It soon disgorged a dozen or so schoolchildren, along with their teacher and chaperones. They had heard about the *Cork Boat* and had come from another village on a field trip to see it.

"They've all seen you on TV," the teacher explained. The kids, all about seven or eight years old, were full of questions. And though I still spoke a fairly fractured Portuguese, I knew enough to understand what they were asking. "How many corks are in the boat? How long did it take to build? Where are you from? Where are you going?"

I answered their questions as best I could, and told them I was about their age when I started saving corks to build the boat, that it had been my dream.

That prompted one boy, who had been staring intently at the boat the whole time, to ask a question of his own.

"How old are you now?"

"Guess," I said.

He wrinkled his forehead, thinking hard. His eyes darted to the boat again, then back to me. Clearly, I must have been saving for years.

"Fifteen?" he ventured. I laughed.

"Thirty-six," I said. His eyes grew wide. I struggled to tell him that he, too, could achieve his dreams if he just stuck with them long enough. His teacher smiled, translating my broken Portuguese.

Then they were off again, laughing and running and tumbling over each other to get back in the minibus and back to school. A field trip to see the *Cork Boat*? We all agreed the children's visit had been a great honor, an homage to the child in all of us. And if we hadn't been turned back by the wind it never would have happened.

Again we settled down to wait. Sometime after lunch I spotted our tow, a low-slung fisherman's boat, putt-putt-putting toward us. At almost the same moment, a speedboat roared into sight from the opposite direction. The speedboat reached the dock first; a middle-aged man, his wife, and son—apparently on vacation—climbed out and tied up.

"Hello," the man said in English, approaching me and extending his hand. "My name is Luis. You are famous."

"Famous?" I said, laughing. "Try stranded." I introduced myself, and explained our trouble with the wind.

"Ah, the wind," he said, knowingly. "It's a problem as ancient as port wine."

"But we have hired a fisherman to tow us through," I said, nodding toward the long blue boat that was slowly approaching, two men aboard. I eyed his Bayliner, with its powerful inboard, with hidden envy.

"How much are they charging?" Luis asked.

I told him. "That's too much," he said, casting a quick glance toward our boat, then his own. "There is no need. We can push you there. . . ."

Push, pull—whatever. He was offering us a tow!

"Are you sure? That's so kind of you! Thank you. But what about the fishermen?" I asked. "We had an agreement. I should pay them something for their trouble, no?"

The fishermen had just cut their engine and were drifting up to the dock. I could see their nets, heaps of fine mesh the color of turquoise piled amidst the thwarts, and a heavy jerrycan of fuel for the return journey.

"You are right. Give them twenty euros," Luis said. "I will explain."

Fifteen minutes later we were under tow, the Bayliner making easy work of the job. Ironically, as we entered the gorge, the water was as smooth as glass—even with our reduced crew we could have made it through, had we known. But so be it; I sat back on a cushioned seat, chatted with Luis and his family, and enjoyed the rugged, magnificent cliffs above us. My obsession with rowing had broken like a fever. A tow? It was all just a part of the journey.

Luis and his family towed us about five miles past the gorge, to a little village, Sra. da Ribeira, that was carved into a steep hillside on the river's north bank. And little was definitely the word. Apart from a small shrine to the Lady of the River, there were only a few houses, a restaurant, and a modest hotel with five rooms. But if the community was little, the view it commanded was as grand and sweeping as any in the world. Great, soaring hillsides scored with terraced vineyards rose to the sky, lining the valley as far as we could see. Across the river, the whitewashed walls of an old *quinta*, or wine estate, stood watch over the valley, its own private chapel topped by a bronze bell.

For once there was no dispute over our schedule. Looking out over the valley, Garth and I declared a rest day. We needed time to relax, review and revise our itinerary, and make small repairs to the boat. We had another reason to stay put, too. We were expecting reinforcements from home: Curtis, who had helped us finish the boat back at the Boat Works; his new girlfriend, Jennifer; and my cousin Tamar.

We were savoring cold beers at sunset and munching cashews on the restaurant's porch when Tamar's cab rolled up. She and I had always been extremely close. When Sara was alive, the three of us had been inseparable. Now, as adults, and especially after Marlene's death, Tamar and I were closer than ever. Since neither of us had siblings, we shared an acute sense that our clan, always important to us, was shrinking. And though she could only take a few days off from her job in New York, there was nothing in the world that would stop her from joining me and my dad on the boat, even if it meant flying overnight to Portugal, rowing for a day and a half, and flying home. Joining us on the *Cork Boat* was an affirmation that, despite her grief, life still held the possibility of joy and excitement.

Tamar was an experienced traveler, but I was still relieved to see her arrive. My instructions had been scant: fly to Porto, call Jorge Osório for an update on where we are, get a cab to the train station, and take the train up the river. Although we weren't quite where we said we would be, she had still managed to catch up with us.

"Everybody in Portugal knows about the *Cork Boat*!" she reported, after we had settled in for dinner. "Even my cab driver from the airport gave me an update."

The next morning, Garth and I set to work on the boat. Overall, it was in pretty good shape, but a few things needed fixing. Despite a liberal application of Vaseline, the centerboard still jammed, and Garth wanted to plane it. Meanwhile, I wanted to fix a few, nascent tessellation problems before they got out of hand. Surveying the entire boat closely from end to end, I found that most of the rubber bands had snapped, as we had anticipated. But for the most part, the netting was still taut, holding the majority of corks in their compact, hexagonal arrays. In a few high-traffic spots, however, where the netting had worked loose, corks had started to pop out of their matrix. At the most basic level, the boat's structural integrity was built upon the uniform, internal order of its corks. Any trouble spot, if left unchecked, could potentially spread to such an extent that the boat's entire structure could collapse into a bundle of loose cork unable to hold its form, decks, or mast. This was unlikely, but with more than half the journey still ahead, we couldn't take any chances.

So I got to work, cinching the slack netting taut again with a back-and-forth bodice of Dacron line that, if a little inelegant, would at least restore the log's hexagonal integrity. It felt great to be working on the boat again, our mooring lines tugging gently at the dock. The magnificent setting was such a contrast to the grimy confines of our garage workshop in that narrow alley now an ocean away.

While we were working, an open launch from Quinta do Vesuvio came roaring across the river, splashing through the rising chop to Sra. da Ribeira. It was Miles Edlmann, the *quinta*'s viticulturalist, whom I'd met the previous afternoon. Enchanted with the *Cork Boat*, he had offered to give us all a personal tour of the winery.

So off we went for an afternoon of libations, drawn from chestnut barrels half the size of a city bus, lined up thirty abreast in a damp, stone warehouse with hand-hewn beams and a dirt floor. It seemed only right, given the viticultural provenance of our boat, that we sample, liberally, the wine from which the Douro drew its identity and vitality.

Quinta do Vesuvio was the sort of estate where heavy doors still creaked open at the turn of a skeleton key, the dining room table sat thirty, and the smoky kitchen boasted a walk-in hearth. It even had its own train station. In the old days, before the railroad, when the port was shipped downriver aboard the *rabelos,* they only filled the casks partway, Miles said. That way, if a boat hit rocks and sank, its precious cargo would float.

As we headed back across the river, a little drunk, the soaking, cold spray brought us back to sobriety. Everyone was still in great spirits, but we had to face the fact that the next day would be a hard one; we would be shoving off well before dawn.

That evening during dinner, I locked eyes with our waitress. "That girl wants to marry you, dude," Garth said as we walked out. "You should go back in there and talk to her."

My confidence, running strong of late, suddenly abandoned me. I could have sworn I was in northern Portugal, but I found myself back in junior high.

"I know, but . . ."

I offered up a list of excuses: I was looking too ratty from the river, my Portuguese wasn't good enough, we had to get up early, her godmother was cooking in the kitchen.

"Oh, just go for it!" he said, walking off. "I'll see you later."

Deep down, I knew he was right. We had spent all those months in the garage, joking about hypothetical maidens along grape-laden riverbanks, building a boat that might never sail. And now, in this little paradise of a village, appeared the very embodiment of maidenhood. Was I going to shove off down the river, never having summoned the courage to walk back through that door?

At that very moment, the restaurant door opened and she stepped outside, flashing me a smile. I was trapped. *"Boa noite!"* I said, mustering my best Portuguese. *"Tens que trabalhar? Ou gosta de ver o barco?"* I think she understood, but I repeated it in English. "Do you have to work? Or would you like to see the boat?" It was a lame pickup line, but the best I could do. We could see the boat from the restaurant; it was only a minute's walk away.

"Sure," she answered, in Portuguese. "Give me a minute."

A few minutes later she emerged, a little dolled up, and we walked down through dusk to the boat.

Our conversation was brief, limited by my lack of Portuguese and her lack of English.

"How old are you?" she asked, as we sat on the boat.

Mentally, I ran through my Portuguese numbers.

"Thirty-six. How old are you?"

"Nineteen."

"I thought you were older," I said.

"How much older?"

I paused, heart pounding, as honesty battled flattery and vultures of guilt began to wheel above.

"Twenty?"

Out of conversation now, we gave up and switched to the international language. Much to our regret, her godmother's sudden appearance on the porch—looking stern and concerned—quickly ended our brief, diplomatic mission. It was dark out, but not that dark. We walked up the hill under her watchful gaze, guilty as charged.

"Boa noite!" I said to the godmother, politely, grateful for once that my limited Portuguese let me escape without further conversation. A last, stolen look into my new friend's deep eyes, and she was gone.

At four-thirty the next morning, Garth and I were down at the boat, strapping on our dry bags and loading bottles of water under the decks. That was the burden and the bounty of being in charge: we tended to take care of the most unpleasant tasks, but we enjoyed that. We were stoics and cheerleaders at once; we did what was necessary and didn't complain.

One by one, the others made their way down to the dock, lugging their gear. With Tamar, Curtis, and Jennifer joining us, we were seven now, and the boat rode lower in the water than I had ever seen. I can't say I contributed much to the load, though. A day earlier, my dry bag had somehow disappeared upriver, reducing me to the shorts I was wearing, an extra T-shirt, a sweatshirt, my journal, and my passport. With a borrowed toothbrush, I had the essentials.

I checked my watch as we pushed off from the dock, under the stars. It was five thirty-seven, a record start for us. As we bent to the oars in silence, pulling through waters black as ink, a faint melody floated after us. It was the village street cleaner, sweeping the pavement in front of the shrine to the Lady of the River. He was singing.

With extra rowers to keep everyone fresh, we made good time toward the Valeira dam. Sometime after nine we began to hear the distant boom of blasting—perhaps highway construction—echoing off the hillsides in an odd, syncopated rhythm. That prompted another one of our many random shipboard discussions, this one about the surrounding geology.

Standing at the tiller as the rest of us, at the oars, faced him, my dad seemed every inch the friendly professor. He noted that the Douro valley was, at a million years old, not even a blink in the four-billion-year history of the earth. And if that history were represented in a single year, he said, Columbus would have made his historic voyage only a moment or two before midnight on December 31.

"We represent just a fleeting second in the life of Earth," he said. "But humans are players now, not just observers. For a long time in evolution, people just reacted to climate and landscape. Now we have the numbers and strength to effect change."

That was evident, on a small scale, along this stretch of the Douro. For centuries, the rocky cataracts of the gorge we were approaching had claimed the lives of many who attempted its passage. Then, in 1780, determined to open the entire river to commerce, Queen Maria ordered her engineers to destroy the biggest of the waterfalls, no matter what it took. Armed with little more than hammers and chisels, hundreds of local workmen attacked the underlying granite. It took eleven years.

Even so, the river wasn't entirely tamed. In 1862, a prominent vintner and port merchant, Baron James Forrester, was sailing through the Valeira gorge after a picnic upstream. On board were several friends, including Antonia Adelaide Ferreira, a powerful vintner in her own right, whose extensive holdings included Quinta do Vesuvio.

Forrester knew the river well; as a young man, he had spent two years living aboard his boat, mapping the river in exquisite detail. But on this particular day the currents betrayed him, and their *barco* was swept into jagged rocks and capsized. Cast into the raging waters, Ferreira and the other women, buoyed up by their billowing skirts, floated to safety. The baron, his money-belt filled with gold, was pulled to the bottom and drowned. Thankfully, we would not be facing such dangers aboard the *Cork Boat,* since the government had dammed the gorge in 1975.

When we arrived at the dam, I scrambled up the adjoining

embankment in search of the lockmaster. Up top, a short, friendly man in a creased uniform emerged from his air-conditioned command post. In addition to requesting passage for the *Cork Boat*, I asked if he would call a cab for my cousin Tamar, who would be getting off the boat. The Valeira dam was only a few miles from the nearest town, and she needed to catch the train back to Porto. Of course, he said.

Over the past week or so, I had grown accustomed to the bizarre nature of our journey, and to the total faith we placed in strangers. Even so, lugging Tamar's suitcase up through the woods to the sunlit road, atop an enormous concrete dam in the middle of nowhere, I was a little reluctant to leave her behind. But these comings and goings were part of the trip; we had to keep moving.

"I'm so glad I came," she said, as we hugged goodbye. For her sake, for Marlene's sake, for my own sake—I was so glad she had come, too. It was an emotional goodbye, not so much for the words exchanged, but for all that was left unspoken. We both knew it was vitally important to keep on living, despite our losses.

Then, with the lockmaster getting impatient, I scrambled down the embankment, cast off, and joined the others in rowing for the nearby lock. Donning orange life jackets for the passage, Garth and I briefed Curtis and Jennifer on the potential maelstrom just ahead. Be ready for hell, we said.

But when the big gate rumbled open, the rowing couldn't have been easier. As the gates closed behind us and the water began to drop, there was an almost sepulchral quality to our descent—the low, metallic whale-song of the mighty floodgates groaning behind us in protest, and the echo of dripping water. It was strangely beautiful sinking deep into the cool shadows, the narrow band of blue sky above shrinking by the second. Up on the lip of the dam, leaning over, was Tamar, whose face got smaller and smaller until she was just a dot.

By late afternoon, our muscles were aching and our blisters oozing, but we kept on rowing. Our sights were set on the next outpost of civilization, the village of Foz Tua. Word on the river was that its café had the best fried fish from here to Porto. More important, it was bound to have cold beer.

We were getting close—Tua was just a mile or so downstream—when we spotted three women on the far bank, waving at us, then yelling. Their voices carried well over the water. "*Cork Boat! Cork Boat!* Stop! Come here! We want to meet you! *Cork Boat!* We want to take a picture with you!"

Was I delirious? Three women in bikinis, begging to meet us? "Hey, guys!" I said. "Let's row over there and take a break!"

For a brief moment nobody answered.

"I have no interest in stopping at this point," Curtis said, casting a sideways glance at Jennifer.

"Yeah—there's beer at the end of this row!" Garth added. Brandt, grumbling about the heat, concurred. "They're too far. Let's keep going."

"Too far?" I answered, incredulous. I could see the women, up on their toes now, waving frantically. "We're fifty strokes from three hot women in bikinis, and they want to meet us. You're telling me we're too far?"

Jennifer laughed, and H, the only married man among us, kept quiet. They weren't getting in the middle of this one.

I pressed my case with the boys. "Come on, you guys. Don't be lame. How many times in your life have three women in bikinis, or three women, period, *begged* to meet you?"

They just shrugged, and kept on rowing.

"Think of Odysseus and the sirens," Brandt ventured, trying to put things in a more positive light. I knew the story: forewarned of beguiling women who lured witless seafarers to their deaths, Odysseus had his crew lash him to the mast so he couldn't steer the ship into danger, no matter how tempted he got. I had brought along a tattered copy of *The Odyssey*, hoping to reread it, but our regimen of near-constant rowing meant the book had remained all but unopened, tucked behind a strap in the bow.

"The lovely voices in ardor appealing over the water made me crave to listen," Odysseus had cried, "and I tried to say 'Untie me!' to the crew, jerking my brows; but they bent steady to the oars. . . . So all rowed on, until the Seirênês dropped under the sea rim, and their singing dwindled away."

However fitting, the Homeric analogy did little to assuage my irritation. But since I was apparently the only one interested in pausing for social pursuits, it wasn't worth starting World War III over. This was a volunteer crew, after all. If they were grumpy and had no interest in stopping, so be it.

"Lame!" I muttered, giving up. "Garth, Brandt—I'll never let you forget this!"

Downriver two days later, we confronted our biggest challenge yet. Checking in with Cork Supply, I learned that the lock at Bagauste, our next dam, was broken. A broken lock meant that nothing could pass the dam except water through the spillways, and even those were shut. Worse yet, it would be at least a week before spare parts arrived from Holland.

We couldn't afford to wait a week. And what if we did and the lock still wasn't fixed? Even though we were tired, sunburned, and sore after a week on the water, we had just started to get a feel for the shifting moods of the river, the rhythms of the wind, and our boat's idiosyncrasies. Yes, our original, confident talk of a leisurely, five-day float through wine country had long since become a wry, running joke, but we had finally—just in the last day or so—started to gain a sense of momentum.

If we found ourselves incredibly frustrated by this latest obstacle, though, we were just as determined to overcome it. Having set our sights on reaching Porto, we would never stop short. Not having come so far. Because, whatever our differences, Garth and I hadn't built the *Cork Boat* as an intellectual exercise; we had built it to make a journey. A journey of folly, perhaps, but a real journey nonetheless. And though I couldn't speak for the others, I knew that Garth, like me, had even come to appreciate the absurd challenge of it all. Deep down, I was glad the Douro was begrudging our progress; it made our voyage all the more satisfying. No, it would take a lot more than a broken lock to keep us from pressing on downriver.

After talking through our limited options, I called Jorge, to summon the truck (loaded with our dollies) so we could haul the boat out and portage around the dam. It was our only choice.

We awoke the next morning to a cold, gray sky—weather to match the task at hand. It was depressing to cut down the rigging, pull the mast, and, waist-deep in water, strap on the cumbersome dollies again. We had anticipated taking the boat out of the water only once, after a final, triumphant row into Porto. Instead we found ourselves emasculating the boat and hauling it onto land just short of our halfway point.

But if portaging the *Cork Boat* seemed an absurd, aggravating necessity, I took solace from the fact that it wasn't the first time that riverine obstacles had forced determined travelers to lug big boats by land. General Charles Gordon—whose swashbuckling adventures in the service of the British Empire were to end, ultimately, at Khartoum with his severed head atop a sharp pike—had once led an expedition up the Nile in search of its fabled source. Confronting the fearsome thunder of the Fola Falls, in remotest Sudan, he wrote: "It was appalling to look at, far less to think of getting anything up or down, except in splinters."

Discouraged but determined to continue, Gordon put a thousand porters to work disassembling the smaller of his steel steamships, the *Nyanza,* a vessel weighing thirty-eight tons. Month after scorching month and screw by rusting screw, they took apart the *Nyanza* and hauled it in pieces overland, around the raging rapids. Once upstream, the boat was reassembled and Gordon pressed onward. Although his quest to discover the river's source was ultimately fruitless, Gordon's logistical prowess was nothing short of spectacular. His portage alone had taken the better part of a year.

By comparison, the *Cork Boat*'s terrestrial detour took only a couple of hours, start to finish. And if we lacked a thousand porters to pull it off, we had Portugal's best hydraulic flatbed. After half an hour's drive, we arrived at the first boat ramp below Bagauste. As it happened, this ramp also happened to be on the outskirts of Régua, our destination for the day.

This particular stop had never really been open to question; the Association of Friends of the Douro River, whose members had welcomed me on that first scouting trip, had promised to give the *Cork Boat* a special welcome here. For all practical purposes, the short row into town would be merely ceremonial, but we were determined to cover the last few hundred yards under our own power.

With the mast back up and the rigging taut, we were just sliding the oars back into their oarlocks when fireworks started going off. Startled, we looked downriver to Régua's not-so-distant quay, where a crowd was gathering. Clearly, this welcome was going to be significantly grander than any of the impromptu salutes we had inspired upriver. We shoved off, pennants snapping in the wind.

The Friends of the Douro had outdone themselves, greeting us quayside with a small, formal ceremony, an honor guard of local police, and copious glasses of vintage port. Even the rain, which began to pelt us in fat drops, couldn't dampen the spirit of welcome.

At a banquet that night in our honor, the songs and the toasts flowed with the wine, and we thanked our hosts profusely for their hospitality. An official from the Dam Authority stood to respond.

"To travel the Douro has always been an adventure," he said solemnly. "From the Romans who came here two thousand years ago to take away wine, to the Moors who traveled to the sea on their own boats of cork, to the *barcos rabelos,* which had to be pulled by thirty men, or oxen. Now you are a part of that history. Now you know—a little bit—the sweat and toil it took to tame this river, and the sacrifice. The river is in your veins now, and you will always be a part of this place."

I had not heard of the Moorish cork boat before, but I took heart from the precedent and from the toast's unabashed sentiment. Still, I slept poorly that night. Perhaps because of the wine, or perhaps because I had not, for once, spent all day rowing myself into exhaustion, I dreamt we were sailing up-river, looking for a broken lock we couldn't find. Then we were rowing hard to nowhere, through water thick as mo-lasses, over and over and over again.

Reality wasn't all that different. Back on the river, we muscled our way slowly westward, day by day. Although Curtis and Jennifer had to leave us in Régua, we were joined, at the same time, by a college buddy of Garth's, an environmental engi-neer named Garvin Heath. Garvin was a big, ebullient guy, well over six feet, and he could pull his weight and then some. Better yet, he was full of good stories.

One tale in particular really captured my imagination, a project he called "Peripatetic Pancakes." A few years earlier, to celebrate his thirtieth birthday, he had hired a mule train to haul four hundred pounds of pancake mix, syrup, jam, skil-lets, fuel, and other supplies a dozen miles into the Sierras of California. There, he set up camp and for the next two weeks cooked free, all-you-can-eat pancakes for any and all passing backpackers.

At first, people were flabbergasted at this unlikely IHOP-in-the-wilderness. Then word started spreading along the trail. One hungry man, a dot-com refugee, stumbled into camp with only a few raisins left. When Garvin welcomed him warmly with unlimited silver-dollar pancakes and a choice of eight toppings, he was practically speechless with gratitude.

Garvin cooked up nearly a thousand pancakes before he ran short of pancake mix and vacation time, and had to head back down the mountain. "It was a phenomenal way to give back to people, and have fun doing it," he explained.

My dad, standing at the tiller, abandoned his usual, quiet reserve. "Garvin, that's just *great*! The next time you do that, let me know. I'd like to come along and help out."

"Absolutely," Garvin said. "You can all come."

I wasn't at all surprised by my dad's enthusiasm. Sunday-morning pancakes had always been a big deal in our house, and he was always at his happiest with spatula in hand, pouring batter onto a sizzling skillet.

And now that I knew a little more about Garvin, I wasn't at all surprised that he'd just flown six thousand miles to help his buddy Garth row the *Cork Boat* down a Portuguese river.

Late one hot afternoon, as we rowed downriver toward an old spa town called Caldas de Aregos, a young woman suddenly appeared from the woods on shore and called out: "Where is John Pollack?"

I almost fell into the water.

"That's me!" I answered, as we rowed toward the bank.

"My name is Ana Paula," she explained, as the boat nosed ashore. "I am a journalist."

She and her cameraman had been trying to track us down all day, in search of an exclusive interview. Could she put Nuno, her cameraman, aboard for the last stretch into Caldas? He was just down the path, at their truck, getting his camera.

"And you?" I asked.

She laughed nervously. "I'm afraid of boats. I will meet you in town."

Lowering our voices, we held a brief conference. We weren't terribly keen on taking reporters aboard, generally speaking. But an extra rower? He could film what he needed and then we'd put him to the oars—fresh muscle for the home stretch.

"Sure, he can come. But he has to help row."

Ana Paula glanced down the path as a burly fellow— evidently Nuno—approached with a bag of gear. She looked back at the boat. She looked at Nuno again. She looked at her watch. I figured she probably had a deadline; putting her cameraman aboard would kill two birds with one stone: great footage and a faster arrival.

"Yes, of course he can row."

And so we welcomed Nuno aboard, careful not to drop his twenty-thousand-dollar camera into the drink. We set him up in the bow, where he could film us rowing, and told him his turn would come shortly. He smiled, a little uncertainly. But when his turn came, he took up the challenge with gusto. He even sang with us as we put him through the paces.

Soon, rounding a bend, the modest town of Caldas came

into sight off to port. By the time we pulled into an empty slip, a small crowd had gathered; among them was Ana Paula. For once we didn't rush to abandon ship in pursuit of the requisite cold beer. In fact, every member of our crew submitted happily to a one-on-one interview, even if they didn't speak Portuguese. After all, we were goodwill ambassadors. Or perhaps it was because Ana Paula was, like many TV reporters, rather attractive. In any case, as suddenly as she had appeared, Ana Paula was gone again—off to file her story.

Although we had come to take the unexpected for granted, the media's sudden appearance really hammered home the strange duality of our trip. Despite the fact that we felt virtually alone on the river, rowing for hours on end without passing so much as a goatherd on the banks, our sense of isolation was really something of an onboard illusion. According to Olga, whom I phoned from the dock, our progress had become a national, even international, story. CNN, BBC, Sky News, the networks—the list went on and on. Her phone had been ringing for days with calls from reporters seeking confirmation of sightings, progress updates, and interviews. Sensitive to intruding too much on our journey, she had been shielding us from the storm, but as we approached Porto, this was getting harder to do. She wanted to know: Would Garth and I be willing to talk with *People* magazine?

An interview with *People* magazine? Standing on the dock in Caldas de Aregos, it all seemed too bizarre. But I could just see it. Three or four years from now, in the waiting room of some dentist in suburban Cleveland, a patient awaiting his second root canal would be flipping through out-of-date magazines and come across the story of the *Cork Boat*. Later, under the influence of laughing gas, the reader might dismiss the memory of that story as some kind of weird hallucination. Sure, we would talk to *People*. Olga gave me the number and I dialed it from the cell.

It was an easy interview, back and forth, until the reporter started to grill Garth. I could only hear Garth's half of the conversation, but, judging from the rising anger in his voice, the reporter was apparently digging for some kind of dirt.

"No. Absolutely not . . ."

"I don't know exactly how many . . ."

"NO! This isn't just some commercial . . ."

"Listen! You'd have to pay me half a million dollars to build . . ."

She kept cutting him off, and by the time he flipped the phone shut, red with frustration, Garth was really riled. Apparently, the reporter had insinuated that the boat was designed from the get-go as a conniving publicity stunt, dreamt up by a cork company. After all, hadn't a cork company given us thousands of corks? Since it seemed like a publicity stunt, she said, *People* probably wouldn't be interested in the story, after all. That was fine by me. We hadn't built the boat to jockey for ink with the latest celebrity wedding or Hollywood romance.

As we pored over the maps that night, it hit us that our journey, which had at times seemed endless, would soon be coming to a close. A few more days of rowing, and we'd be in Porto. In one sense, we couldn't wait. We were all exhausted, and looking forward to a big celebration at the finish. Getting down the river was our goal, and to achieve it after such a hard slog would surely be satisfying beyond measure. But our pending finish also posed a bigger, more personal question: What would come next? It would be hard to top this trip.

At a bar down by the Caldas waterfront, I struck up a late-night conversation with the gruff captain of the *Douro Acima,* one of the smaller, *rabelo*-style tour boats that had passed us on the river several times. His name was Luis Candido; he and his first mate were heading to Porto with an empty vessel.

"Why don't you just let me give you a tow to the dam?" he asked. "It will go faster."

"That is very generous," I answered. "But rowing makes us strong." I flexed my biceps with a grin.

Captain Candido's eyes narrowed. He was a short, wiry man with a deeply lined face. A blue vein meandered across his bald pate, pulsing at his temple. He had clearly spent years on the river, and perhaps for him it was no longer a sentimental journey.

"But it will take you four hours to the dam!" he insisted. "And at midday the lock will be jammed with boats—you'll never get through."

I could tell he meant well, but he couldn't quite comprehend my refusal. As he saw it, what was the point of rowing when you didn't have to? It just didn't make sense.

"Listen," I said. "We'll race you—the *Cork Boat* against the *Douro Acima*."

He scoffed.

"I'm serious. We'll leave at five-thirty. You leave at eleven-fifteen. We'll beat you to the dam."

Despite his best efforts to scowl again, a grin spread across his face.

"We'll pass you coming and going," he said. The race was on.

In all fairness, there would be no contest whatsoever without that head start. His was an eighty-foot boat with an inboard engine the size of a small hippopotamus. The competition, though, was a good thing. It would spur us on in the morning, when we needed extra motivation. What time was it, anyway? I looked at my watch: nearly midnight. Yes, I would definitely need that motivation.

"We'll see you at the dam," I said.

Garth and I were down at the boat before even the slightest hint of dawn, stowing sandwiches and water for the day and strapping on gear. We shoved off at just after five-thirty into wraithlike mist. Despite our stiffness and the damp morning chill, the early start felt good. Still a little sleepy, we were all more apt to think than talk, pulling through the glassy waters in silent unison. Astern, as the deep blue of night slowly gave way to the pink smudge of dawn, my dad stood at the tiller, calm as ever. How many days had we been on the river? I couldn't quite remember anymore. I didn't even know what day it was.

And then it struck me. It was July 13, his birthday. "Hey, H—happy birthday!"

"It's your birthday, Hank?" Garth asked, as the others chimed in. "How old?"

"Sixty-six."

We all agreed that he was doing pretty well for a guy his age, navigating a cork boat down a river in Portugal. But who could have predicted such an odd birthday?

It was just after nine when we heard the distant, approaching throb of an engine. Upriver, a glassy braid of wake rolled from behind a bend, followed momentarily by a big yellow *rabelo:* it was the *Douro Acima,* in hot pursuit. So much for our five-hour head start. He had left early.

Soon upon us, the *Acima* cut its engine. Grinning, Captain Candido emerged from the wheelhouse.

"Reboque?" he yelled, line in hand. Need a tow?

"Não," I answered. It had become our little joke. *"Precisas que te reboque?"* Do *you* need a tow?

He shook his head. *"Café?"*

Hot coffee was an offer we couldn't refuse. Tying the *Cork Boat* alongside, we clambered aboard his vessel, where the first mate already had a pot brewing.

"It's my father's birthday," I announced.

"Really?" Luis asked. "Let's eat some cake."

And a cake he produced—half a sheet of chocolate, with white frosting. At that, we all broke into a spirited rendition of "Happy Birthday"—half in English, half in Portuguese—as my dad grinned.

"JP, you pulled it off again," he said, as we untied the *Cork Boat* and resumed our journey. "Another river, another cake."

Though I couldn't really claim credit for this morning's cake, I knew what he meant. He was talking about another of his birthdays, many summers earlier, when I had been his field assistant in Botswana. We had spent that day in the bowels of a copper mine—a dark, hot, warren of dangerous shafts roaring with pneumatic drills. Changing levels meant climbing through steel conduits that doubled as drains. Water rushed past just inches from my headlamp as I stepped, tentatively, from one slippery rung to the next.

That night, not far from the mine, we camped on the dry riverbed of the Limpopo River. It was pretty bleak there, the banks tangled with thorny underbrush and the sand underfoot laced with dung and the tracks of foraging hyenas. After a simple dinner around our campfire, I brought out a Sara Lee birthday cake. I had bought it in the mine's commissary, and snuck it back to camp.

Nearly two decades had passed in a flash. And here we were again—another river, another birthday, another unexpected chocolate cake. It was rich.

Reunion

As we drew closer and closer to Porto, we marveled at our apparent celebrity. Mayors along the river now sent boats out to greet us, and restaurants refused to let us pay. Passing trains blew their whistles in salute, as passengers leaned from the windows, cheering. Townspeople gathered at the docks to give us gifts for the journey—a loaf of crusty bread, a ham, a bag of yellow plums, a bottle of homemade port. One little girl, whose mom nudged her forward with encouragement, nervously presented us with a bouquet of sunflowers.

All this attention was at once gratifying and a little embarrassing. We hadn't started out with any pretensions of celebrity. But now that we were so well known, and flying the American flag, we felt like de facto American ambassadors.

"For centuries," said the mayor of Bitetos, a small town not far from Porto, "thousands and thousands of Portuguese have left their homes in search of work, traveling the world in search of opportunity. Nowhere have they been more warmly received than in America. Today, we are honored to welcome you in return, to show you that same hospitality."

And he did, organizing a banquet, putting us up for the night at a hilltop *quinta,* and sending a vintage Mercedes limo to ferry us back to the boat.

On our last truly lazy, midday drift, we laid out a veritable feast on the deck—meat, cheese, fruit, and a bottle of port to pass and swig despite the hot sun. This was the leisurely, decadent float through wine country that I had always imagined.

That afternoon, while docked for a rest at a crowded beach, I looked across the river to see a white powerboat heading straight for us. As it drew closer, a familiar figure appeared in the bow, waving. It was my mom! She was back in Portugal to join us for the home stretch.

She had said she was planning to return for the grand finale, but we didn't know exactly when we'd see her. Like Tamar, she had found us on the river, and I was really proud. Not so much that she had been able to track us down—I knew she would—but that she had the desire, spirit, and will to make her second trip to Portugal in less than three weeks, just to celebrate the culmination of her son's boyhood dream.

Watching her approach, it struck me that not every mom would have volunteered to help her depressed, unemployed, adult son assemble corks in a leaky garage, just to lift his flagging spirits and keep his quirky project alive. Not every mom would have appreciated the sublime possibilities of such an absurd endeavor, or why it was important that we share it as a family. Somehow, I had gotten very lucky in the mom department. Three decades earlier, she had helped nurture the *Cork Boat*'s very beginning; now she would be there to celebrate its triumphant end.

When the boat reached us, my dad and I each grasped one of her forearms to help her onto the dock. As the three of us hugged, the people who had ferried her across the river motored off again, to our belated shouts of *"obrigado!"*

If only a dozen days had passed since we parted on the cobbled streets of Foz Côa, it felt like a month. Dark from the sun and perhaps a little cocky from our hard-fought pull down the river, we were no longer the shell-shocked crew she had left behind, wondering how we would ever make it to Porto.

We were weary, yes, and nursing our respective injuries—Brandt's sore elbow; Garth's and Garvin's blisters (bandaged with duct tape); H's swollen knee; and my shoulders, which for several days had been clicking painfully with every stroke. But we were confident now, and getting so close to the end we could almost taste the sweet salt of the sea.

Reunited, we all boarded the *Cork Boat* and shoved off, on down the river. Later, while the others dove into the water for a swim, my mom suddenly smiled and said, "JP, do you realize that this is the first time your father has joined you on one of *your* expeditions, instead of vice versa?"

I hadn't thought of it that way. The realization made me

proud, but also a little rueful. I was getting older, and so was my dad.

We tied up that night at a marina just above the river's final dam, guests of our friends Luis and Su Reyes, who had towed us through that windy gorge below Foz do Sabor. It was a private yacht club, but they had cleared our stay with the manager. The night watchman would keep an eye on the *Cork Boat* for us—not a bad idea, now that we were on the very outskirts of Porto itself. It felt strange to catch a cab downtown for dinner—the same downtown with which I had become so familiar during my preparations for our journey. It all seemed different now: bigger, louder, so busy and brash compared to the quiet vineyards upriver.

A day or two earlier, Garth had been adamant: "I don't want to even see Porto until we row into town," he insisted. I felt exactly the same way. We wanted a clean, clear finish, not some gradual, multi-day arrival, anticlimactic for its attenuation. No, we wanted to make a splash.

Reluctantly, though, we had come to the conclusion that, given our limited speed on the river and the requirements of a scheduled, ceremonial arrival, we had little choice but to position the boat for a short, final sprint on the last day. If there was one thing the river had taught us over the past couple of weeks, it was respect for Mother Nature. If we risked a long, hard row into the city on our final day, we might well miss our own party.

And according to Olga it was going to be a big party. Press calls were coming in from all over the world. The mayors of Porto and Vila Nova de Gaia—fierce political rivals who often battled for the limelight—had both inquired about offering the official welcome, and several port houses were reportedly vying for a role in the celebration. There was so much interest in the *Cork Boat*'s arrival, in fact, that Cork Supply had decided to organize a press conference aboard one of Douro Azul's big riverboats, which would meet us midstream. That way, all the photographers and TV camera crews could film us rowing across the finish line with the old, picturesque port warehouses in the background.

If the trip had been ours, then the finish belonged to all those who had helped make our trip such a success, not just in the United States, but in Portugal. A lot of people had invested time and energy and enthusiasm in our voyage, and we owed them a grand arrival, one they could share in and savor, too. And so we took the snarled rush-hour traffic, honking horns, and hustle and bustle of Porto in stride, settling in at a crowded, casual restaurant for a low-key dinner. Late that night, back in our hotel, my dad pulled our tattered, dog-eared maps from their tube and unrolled them on his bed. Everybody loved those map meetings, and this would be one of our last. I loved them for the aching progress we could chart. I loved them for the inherent promise of progress to come. I loved them because, no matter how tough the river really was, those maps made long miles look short, the journey ahead as easy as the sinuous sweep of a blue highlighter across smooth paper.

Whether we unfurled them on a windy, rocking deck in a choppy gorge, or spread them out on a hotel mattress in downtown Porto, studying the maps always brought us together as a team. If we had questions or disagreements or preferences, we would talk them through. The map meetings were all about camaraderie.

As he flipped each sheet over in turn, the winding Douro unfolded before us, meandering from Barca de Alva through Foz Côa . . . Foz do Sabor . . . Sra. da Ribeira . . . Foz Tua . . . Pinhão . . . Régua . . . Mesão Frio . . . Caldas de Aregos . . . Bitetos . . . Finally, we had reached the last of our twelve maps. At the right edge was the final dam, at Crestuma. At the left edge, the Atlantic Ocean. In between, the river swept to the sea in a great, curving S that separated the city of Porto, on the north bank, from Vila Nova de Gaia, on the south. In preparing the maps back in Ann Arbor, my dad had marked our finish with a bright orange slash across the river itself. We were almost there. One last time we chose a destination—a dock within a mile or so of the finish. We would tie up there for the night, setting ourselves up for an easy, ceremonial arrival the final day.

Rowing out of our slip at dawn to the applause of a small knot of well-wishers, we hailed a passing sand-and-gravel freighter whose captain agreed to let the *Cork Boat* share his scheduled passage through the dam. Juxtaposed with the freighter in the lock's tight confines, the *Cork Boat* looked lilliputian. And to the burly, tattooed sailors watching us from the ship's battered fantail, we must have seemed a motley crew: not only were our T-shirts soiled, stained, and greasy with the Vaseline we used to lube the centerboard, but we had mistakenly purchased a tube of sunscreen meant for kids, and our arms, legs, and faces were covered with purple glitter. We looked absolutely ridiculous; all we could do was laugh.

When the downriver sluice-gate opened, the freighter, prop thrashing, rumbled out of the lock and off on down the river. Relieved to be past the final dam of our journey, we rowed confidently into the home stretch. Another ten miles, and we'd be in downtown Porto. Congratulating each other, we stowed oars, shed our life jackets, and pulled out the maps for a look at what lay between us and our night's mooring.

And then, while studying the maps, we noticed something: we were drifting. For the first time since we had launched the boat in Barca de Alva, a steady current was carrying us downstream. Freed from the confines of its last dam, the river was finally flowing to the sea. And after nearly a hundred and thirty miles of hard rowing, we were flowing with it. We cheered like the aching, weary rowers that we were. An actual current? On this stubborn river that had seemed so determined to deny us passage?

H pulled out the GPS to calculate our speed. Sure enough, we were clipping along at over two knots, without so much as rowing a stroke. Luxuriating in gravity's sudden generosity, we hoisted sail to catch the last of the morning breeze, and steered for Porto.

It was a glorious, cloudless day, one like so many others before it. But in just a few hours, only our victory lap would remain. And so we took our time, playing about and pausing at one point to "race" a group of kids who paddled out to greet us in their kayaks. They beat us handily, laughing. We rewarded them by tossing out some of our custom-made souvenir corks, the ones bearing our endeavor's tag line— "165,321 Corks. 1 Boat."

And then, as if to remind us who was boss one last time, the wind started to shift. Of course it shifted; it always did in the afternoon. If we dawdled at midday, we paid the price later. Laughing, we dropped the luffing sail and took up the oars. We could see our day's goal, the first of Porto's six bridges, about a mile downstream. The public dock we were aiming for would be just a couple hundred yards past it, off to port. We pulled steadily, in practiced unison. We were almost there.

Or were we? The harder we rowed, the less progress we

seemed to be making. I checked our pennants. The breeze was stiff against us, but not *that* stiff. We'd overcome much stronger winds upstream. But the river, judging from floating debris, was now flowing upstream and gaining strength with every passing minute. What was going on?

"It's the tide," my dad announced, suddenly. "It's coming in." Of course! Our morning's free ride below the last dam hadn't just been the river's natural flow to the sea. It was the morning ebb tide. Now the tide had turned against us, and hard. But if the river wanted to challenge us one last time, we would show it who was boss.

Our yells of macho defiance soon gave way to a determined silence as Garth, Garvin, Brandt, and I leaned back into every stroke, pulling harder now than we had the entire trip. It was apparent that we couldn't afford to waste a single stroke, or take even a short breather. If we rested for more than a moment, the surging tide would send us racing back upriver.

"What's it look like ahead, Lana?" Garth called out to my mom, who was up in the bow. Rowing, we had an excellent view of where we'd end up if we gave up the fight.

"There's a buoy about twenty yards ahead," she answered.

"Let's just get there and tie up," I said.

At the tiller, my dad was already steering the course. "That's where we're headed," he said.

If the rowing was hard before, now it turned brutal. Every single stroke was a contest of wills, one that pitched our screaming muscles and tendons and sinews against the inexorable, ferocious tide. Off to starboard, I could hear a man yelling *"Cork Boat! Cork Boat! Cork Boat!"* but couldn't afford to look. I had to stay focused on the red blade of my oar, cutting through water that felt as thick as wet cement.

The sheer physical demand of it all triggered memories of a brutal cross-country meet my senior year in high school, against our crosstown rival. As I was struggling uphill with a half-mile to go, a lanky runner in the hated purple-and-white jersey had pulled even with me, gunning for the finish. His coach, who had the reputation of a slave driver, was screaming at the kid, "How bad do you want it! How bad do you want it!"

Through our labored breathing, I overheard my rival mutter "Fuck you"—not at me, but at his coach. Stride for painful stride now, I dug into the hill with my last reserves, driven by anger and fear. If I wasn't a yard or two ahead by the top, I'd never be able to match his long legs on the downhill sprint to the finish. It was now or never.

But the bastard hung with me, right on my shoulder, step after step. The last hundred yards of that race were pure agony, pain distilled to its purest form. With nothing left, I willed my legs into a panicked, determined sprint, spikes cutting into the dry turf with a fury I had never before tapped. Every fiber of my body screamed in protest, but there could be no surrender. I beat that guy across the line by two steps.

That race had taken place nineteen years earlier, and until now I had never pushed myself to such an extreme. Stroke by agonizing stroke, we pulled on those oars with everything we had, their long, carbon-fiber shafts arching from the strain and almost lifting us from the decks. Up in the bow, my mom shouted encouragement, calling off our progress as we muscled forward. The hard truth was that in the last fifteen minutes of all-out rowing, we had barely covered fifteen yards.

"We're going to have one shot at this buoy," my dad said as we inched within the last few yards. "I'll steer us past, and when I give the word, Garth will get to the bow and make the throw as we drift back. JP, you get up there, too, ready to help."

The water was literally racing past us, sucking at the boat with determined fury as we clawed our way past the green steel buoy, itself straining at its anchor chain. Given the length of our oars, we had to give it wide berth. At my dad's signal, Garth made his move, darting to the bow as Garvin and Brandt yanked in the starboard oars, getting them out of the way. Oars clear, my dad shoved the tiller to port, and we began to swing fast, toward the buoy.

In a few seconds we were there. Garth dropped a tight double loop over the top and braced himself against the bow as the line played out. In another instant, the buoy would be yanked flat in the water.

"My wrist!" Garth yelled. It was caught in the line.

Already at his shoulder, I reached over for the tangled mooring line and pulled with the strength of pure adrenaline. Together, with three hands, the two of us managed to gain just enough slack for him to free his other hand, unhurt.

Arm over arm now, our feet slipping against the boat's wet netting, we strained to reel in six feet of extra line. We were essentially towing three thousand pounds against the tide with our arms alone, but we had little choice. We had to tie the boat more securely or risk jerking loose. If we came loose, we would rocket upriver in disarray, oars akimbo, unable to do anything but settle for an unceremonious beaching.

Together we managed, barely. But now what? Our destination—our mooring for the night—wasn't far. In fact, we could see it clearly, just a few hundred yards away. But it might as well have been miles. Because even if we were able to row with the same intensity we had mustered to cover the past twenty yards, it would take five hours, at that same rate, to cover the distance. It was a physical impossibility.

And then I remembered something. Weeks earlier, leaving my meeting at Douro Azul, Pedro Negrão had handed me two pages, dense with figures: the tide tables for the Douro estuary in June and July.

"Hey! We've got tide tables! They're in H's bag."

I retrieved them, and my dad, who had studied such tables during one summer as an ROTC midshipman aboard the battleship USS *Wisconsin*, quickly determined the hard truth: the tide would be running against us for the next five hours. This left us four options—row like madmen for another five hours, wait at the buoy until the tide turned, retreat upriver for a familiar, five-hour row in the morning, or hail a tow.

The thought of hailing a tow for the last, lousy two hundred yards—within Porto city limits, no less—stung our pride. But given our choices, it seemed like the best option. We were debating it unhappily, passing a water bottle around, when a little red boat came chugging upriver. It was a man and two little boys, out fishing.

"There's our tow!" I said. "Should we flag them down?"

Garth looked at his watch. It was going on four o'clock.

"Yeah, let's do it," he said.

So we flagged them down, and when they motored close, I explained our little problem, which was probably both obvious and funny—funny, that is, if you hadn't just rowed for sixteen days. As I talked, I sized up his boat. It was home-built, with only a twenty-horse outboard. Was that little engine strong enough to tow us against the current? I wasn't sure. Our boat was yanking on that steel buoy like an angry bull.

But it wasn't my call. I pointed to the marina, back to the bow of the *Cork Boat,* and then to his craft, and popped the big question: *"Reboque?"*

"Sim," he said, nodding. "Throw me a line."

Not wanting to untie from the buoy until we were safely secured to his boat, we decided to reposition our stern line, attaching it to the towing harness up front. Once again, I was grateful for Garth's facility with knots. He was in his element, reddish hair glinting in the sun, his bony hands moving with the confidence born of a hundred hard climbs.

When everything was ready and our lines were in order, I waved the all clear. Nodding, the fisherman goosed his engine, a blue cloud of exhaust rising in protest. For a moment, we went nowhere. But sure enough, at full throttle, his boat could pull us slowly forward.

In just a few minutes, we passed under the bridge, out of the fierce channel, and into the marina. A small crowd of onlookers had gathered and, despite rumors of a rough neighborhood, they seemed as curious and friendly as their compatriots upriver, eager to lend a hand. A short, wiry fellow named Gerónimo identified himself as the marina's night watchman.

"Your boat will be safe here," he assured us. "I will watch it."

For our benefactor in the little red boat, I reached blindly belowdecks to our "bar" and came up with a bottle of Jack Daniels. We had been given so many bottles of port and liquor over the past few days that we could never drink them all. Though he accepted the bottle with a smile, he brushed aside our thanks. "It was nothing," he insisted.

Exhausted, we lugged the oars and the life jackets and remaining gear up to Gerónimo's house, overlooking the dock. Afterward, over bottles of cold beer in a nearby café, we reveled in our good luck—not only in the help we had received from freighter to dory to dock, but in having to confront the brutal afternoon current. If we hadn't been delayed in getting through the dam, we would never have discovered the terrible strength of the incoming tide. And since we were scheduled to cross the finish line the next day at two-thirty P.M.—into the tide's teeth, according to our tables—we now had time to come up with an alternate plan.

Again we pulled the maps from their battered cardboard tube. Given the incoming tide, there was no way we could row downriver in the afternoon. But a quick call to Cork Supply confirmed what I suspected: rescheduling our arrival was impossible, too. Olga had already notified every news outlet in Portugal, and then some. Still, tide or no tide, there was absolutely no way we would accept a tow across the finish line.

We argued back and forth about what to do. Then my dad, ever the quiet champion of cunning over brute strength, proposed an elegant solution. Pointing to the very edge of the final map, he suggested we catch the morning wind and tide for an easy jaunt to the very mouth of the Douro. Yes, we would pass the finish line hours early. And then, after tying up for lunch, we could catch the incoming tide and the afternoon wind to sail upriver, *back* to the finish.

Catch the cursed afternoon wind to complete our journey? It would be only too sweet.

Our penultimate night was one of total exhaustion. The river had wrung us out like rags. A leisurely float through wine country? It had been a battle all the way. And on the eve of our grand arrival, it was all we could do to drag ourselves to dinner with Jorge, near the hotel.

Though enthusiastic about our arrival, Jorge relayed some jarring news: the night before, Francisco Pinto, Cork Supply's sales chief, had been held up at gunpoint outside his apartment by two toughs on motorbikes. A pistol at his temple, he had been stripped of his wallet, passport, and other valuables.

My stomach tightened. "Is he okay?"

"Yes, but he was very frightened," Jorge answered, adding that stickups just didn't happen very often in Portugal. Not with guns, anyway.

The robbery was a harsh reminder of the real world we had left behind for the past two and a half weeks, and I found myself wondering if, now that we were back in the big city, the boat would be vandalized. I just had to trust that the night watchman would not fall asleep.

After dinner, with everyone dragging from our day's exertions, we walked back to the hotel. Lying in bed, I struggled to capture the day's events by writing, as I always did, in my journal. But after forcing out a few cursory lines I let my pen drop, swept away by a flood of thoughts. I thought of how much I had come to loathe collecting corks, but also of the friends I had made doing it. I thought of the exhaustion and excitement of working through the final night with so many volunteers in Garth's alley, against hope and the clock, struggling to finish the boat. I thought of the frustration of the dry launch, and the triumph I felt upon seeing the boat splash into the Potomac for the first time. I thought, too, of all that we had experienced in the past weeks. Even now, on the verge of finality, the whole experience seemed wildly improbable, and all the better for it.

But as hard as I had pushed to build the boat, get it over to Portugal, and make it down the river, our pending arrival suddenly didn't seem to matter quite as much as it had. Sure, it would be exciting. But it was the getting here, in the broadest sense, that had been so perfect. And it wasn't perfect because I was able to forget all the anger, the sadness, the clash of egos, the doubt and frustration that had plagued me as I pursued this crazy project. It was perfect because I could finally accept all that, even embrace it.

I thought of Garth in all his generosity, his brilliance, and his sometimes debilitating perfectionism. Our friendship had flowed so easily before I had asked him to join me on the boat project. Now the cross-currents of our friendship were far more complex. Our admiration for each other was surely greater than ever, but it was also tempered by deep, private frustrations and no small amount of anger on both our parts. How could I love him and want to throttle him at the same time? But we had made the project work, because we were, for better or worse, in the same boat, literally and figuratively. Ultimately, the *Cork Boat* and I were both stronger and better for Garth's stubbornness. Maybe our friendship would be, too.

I thought, too, of Sara, and how in many ways my childhood had died with her. Yes, I had ultimately hung on to a spirit of play, somehow determined to squeeze some joy from the rinds of grief. But for so long my life had been just that—

an exercise in determination. Yes, in the decades since I saw her drown, I had gained enough time to recover, but never quite to heal. Deep down, I had always felt cheated of my childhood, and in saving corks all these years to build the boat, perhaps I had been trying to hang on to a happier, more innocent past.

For some reason, it had taken me a long time to realize that grief and happiness, frustration and satisfaction, anger and love, didn't cancel each other out. Now I finally knew I could only counterbalance my deepest losses and hardest times by savoring the good times all the more. But I would always have to live with both.

Growing drowsy now, my thoughts wandered to one of my favorite childhood bedtime stories, a book called *Paddle-to-the-Sea.* Richly illustrated, it follows the voyage of a little wooden Indian in a carved toy canoe that drifts—over many years and with occasional help—from the north shore of Lake Superior, through every one of the Great Lakes, and out the Saint Lawrence to the Atlantic. At the end of the book, the Indian boy who first carved the craft, by now a man, learns by chance that his beloved Paddle-to-the-Sea had finally fulfilled the journey of his childhood imagination.

Although I wasn't sure exactly when my own journey had, in all its many dimensions, begun, I knew for certain that its end was fast approaching. Not that life wouldn't offer me other grand adventures, but I would surely never experience another journey quite like that of the *Cork Boat*. It was a bittersweet feeling.

And then this tide of swirling emotion began to ebb into sleep. Determined to write just a little bit more, I mustered the dregs of my discipline to pen one last line in my journal. "End in sight," I scrawled, and sank into slumber.

OCEAN

The next morning, when our taxi dropped us at the dock, our night watchman, Gerónimo, was nowhere to be found. Yet we had no complaints: not only was the *Cork Boat* safe from harm, but he had laid our long oars out neatly on the dock, their glossy red blades gleaming in the sunshine. This was it. The final day. The end of the journey.

After fitting the boat with a couple of Cork Supply banners and donning new CORK BOAT T-shirts, we took to the river late in the morning, hoisting sail as soon as we were clear of the dock. There were seven of us aboard: Garth and I, my parents, Brandt, Garvin, and, for the first time, Jorge. But even heavily laden, the boat moved more swiftly than it ever had before, coursing downriver with ease. And although it wasn't necessary, we rowed. Not out of habit, but out of pride.

The city rose on either side—steep, jumbled hillsides of cobbled alleyways and old houses, their iron balconies bedecked with flowers and fluttering with laundry. One by one, we passed beneath the city's soaring bridges, chasing our own shadow downriver, toward the finish. As we approached the Luis Primeiro bridge, our designated finish line, I took the tiller from H.

The others whooped as we began to sweep under its mighty span, blasting the air horn we had carried for emergencies, and trumpeting a rather nasal rendition of Handel's *Water Music* on kazoos. A passing riverboat let loose with its horn, too.

Alone in my thoughts amidst all this hubbub, I just tried to drink up the moment in all its glory. No cheer could express the utter satisfaction I felt, or the profound sense of personal triumph. What had started with a single cork—an idea, really—had finally come to this. None of it had been inevitable, or even remotely likely.

My momentary reverie was broken as the now-familiar chant rose from the boat and I joined in, our voices echoing from the steel truss-work soaring above us: *"Cork Boat! Cork Boat! Cork Boat! Cork Boat!"*

Jubilant, we sailed onward toward Foz, the mouth of the Douro. An hour later, rounding the river's final bend, we suddenly caught sight of a bright blue horizon stretching off a sandy spit to infinity—the Atlantic Ocean.

"Let's keep going!" Garth yelled.

We all laughed. In truth, the boat might almost have been strong enough. Its crew was definitely not. We set course, instead, for the wharf at Afurada, a little village on the south side of the river. There, dozens of local fishermen had lashed their colorful dories, four and five abreast, against a stone sea-wall. Many of the boats were filled to the gunwales with nets the color of green sea foam, redolent with the smell of fish. As gulls wheeled through the blue sky, swooping and squabbling over the remains of the day, we tied up our wine-cork folly to its hard-working cousins and scrambled onto the pier.

A welcoming committee from Cork Supply was there to greet us, among them our patron Jochen Michalski, who had made the whole trip possible, and Francisco. Shaken but unhurt from his brush with the robbers, Francisco had already recovered his sense of humor.

"The worst of it was the article in the newspaper today!" he chortled. "It said a 'middle-aged man was robbed at gun-point.' *Me? Middle-aged?*"

"Only chronologically," I assured him. "You still have a boy's spirit!"

And he did. I thought of his dog-eared copy of *Kon-Tiki,* and of my own. Adulthood be damned; the *Cork Boat* had proven that age was just a state of mind.

At a small restaurant overlooking the wharf, we sat down to lunch and waited for the tide to turn. After the requisite round of toasts, I told Jochen I had a question to ask.

"Whatever inspired you to send thousands of corks to some guy you didn't even know who claimed to be building a cork boat?"

He paused for a moment. "It was just such a great idea," he said. "It didn't matter to me if it had any commercial value. I never expected all of this attention. I just thought that if you were willing to build it, the least I could do was help out with a few corks."

"Just a few," I said. He laughed.

And then my dad pointed to his watch. The tide would be turning any minute and it was time to go.

Masters of the river now, we had timed our return perfectly. By the time we got back down to the boat, both the wind and the tide had shifted in our favor. And as we cruised easily upriver under full sail, the hoopla began in earnest. There were big riverboats, lined with cheering passengers and blasting their horns in salute. There was Captain Candido of chocolate cake fame, grinning aboard a crowded *Douro Acima,* holding up a coil of tow rope and shouting, *"Reboque?"* There were cars honking from the shore. And there was the little boat that had rescued us from the last buoy; the man had motored out with his sons again, to welcome us. Overhead, a press helicopter swooped low and banked back, a cameraman leaning out its open door for dramatic aerial footage. Aboard *Millenium,* one of the Douro Azul's big riverboats, dozens of reporters and camera crews crowded the rails, recording our arrival for posterity.

We put on a smart show for them, our red blades pulling through the water in a precise parallel rhythm, broken only when we stopped to wave. For the first time in the entire voyage, I was sorry to be making such good time; this victory lap was so easy and so much fun that I didn't want it to end. But as we drew close to the soaring bridge, my dad steered us, finally, toward our appointed terminus on the waterfront of Vila Nova de Gaia, where a dozen *barcos rabelos* lay at anchor.

At the last possible moment I dropped the sail, and the *Cork Boat* drifted to a gentle stop at *Millenium*'s stern. Standing in the bow, I tossed a line to a uniformed crewman, and scrambled aboard to tie us up. Knotting the line securely, I tried to ignore the whirring and clicking and flashing of cameras, some just inches from my face, but I couldn't stop grinning.

The mayor of Vila Nova de Gaia was on deck to greet us. I had been joking all morning that we might be given the key to the city. I wasn't far off. He gave us what might be described as the key to the city's heart—bottles of vintage port. Presenting them, he gave me a gifted politician's conspiratorial wink. "Nineteen ninety-two," he said. "A very good year!"

In order to satisfy all the national and international media, Olga had organized a press conference in the ship's lounge. Garth and I flanked the mayor and Jochen at a table in front, facing a half-dozen television cameras, six or eight photographers, a clutch of reporters, and a lot of familiar faces from up and down the river. There was Su, who with her husband, Luis, had towed us through the windy gorge below Foz do Sabor. Several of our friends from Régua had made the trip down to Porto, as well. Next to them was the mayor of Bitetos, who had also welcomed us with fireworks and a banquet. António, our singing truck driver, was there, and in the back of the room . . . Yes! It was my beautiful waitress from

Sra. da Ribeira! And drats—there was her godmother, standing watch. Most of Cork Supply seemed to be there, too—they must have shut down operations for the day. It struck me suddenly that outside of my parents, Brandt, and Garth, I had known none of these people a month earlier. Now, it seemed, I knew half of Portugal.

As I adjusted the bouquet of microphones before me and waited for the mayor to begin, my mind flashed back for an instant to Capitol Hill. How many times had I stood at the back of the room, listening to members of Congress holding forth? How many times had I heard others speaking words I had written for them? Suddenly it felt a little strange to be up front, at the center of the storm, speaking for myself.

The mayor opened the press conference by welcoming us to Vila Nova de Gaia, noting that the *Cork Boat* "proves that you don't have to cause a stock market crash or be a terrorist to make the news." Jochen followed up by presenting Garth and me with remarkably detailed scale models of the *Cork Boat*, hand-crafted by Portugal's leading cork modeler. I looked at Jorge, who was grinning at the back of the room. These models had been his idea, something to commemorate our journey. They were practically perfect replicas of our vessel, rendered in cork, right down to the long oars. Examining my model, it occurred to me it was a toy of a toy—though hardly a toy at all. That modeler and I, we had taken our respective toy boats very seriously.

And then it was my turn, to speak on behalf of the *Cork*

Boat crew. I looked out at my parents, beaming in their folding chairs behind all the photographers and camera crews. If my mom had taught me one lesson as a boy—a lesson later hammered home by years in politics—it's that you can never say thank you enough. And that's how I started. Speaking in English, I thanked them for their love and faith in me—and for saving corks all those years. The audience laughed. Somehow, they were all with me, emotionally. I choked up for a moment, thinking of Marlene and Sara. How could I feel both loss and joy at once? But as I forced myself to press on with my thanks—and then our story—I regained my footing.

The questions that followed came fast and furious, but they were mostly familiar. "What was your inspiration? Did you ever doubt you would make it? Why did you choose Portugal? What was the most difficult moment? What do you think of the Portuguese people?" I took some of the questions and Garth took others. It was fun talking about the boat, and we took our time. Nobody seemed in a hurry to go, not even the TV crews, with their perpetual deadlines.

Then, just as things were winding down, there came one last question. "Where will you sail the *Cork Boat* on its next voyage?"

I paused. The truth was, I didn't think there would ever be a next voyage. Not because the boat wasn't up to it. But the voyage of the *Cork Boat* had been the journey of a lifetime, quite literally. Its magic came from the richness of context. From geography, history, and the sheer novelty of the adventure. From its roots in a boy's dream, and from all the people who, through the years and over the miles, had lent a hand to make that dream come true. I couldn't say it aloud—not here, at least—but the *Cork Boat* would probably never sail again.

The room was quiet, waiting for an answer.

"Its next voyage?" I said. "Right now we're too tired to think about that. And we're still savoring this one. So to everyone who made it possible—*muito obrigado!*"

And then it was over, and people drifted out. After some lingering conversations and a last bottle of beer on deck, my parents, Garth, Brandt, Garvin, and I climbed aboard the *Cork Boat* one last time and shoved off. Settling in at the oars, we rowed across the river toward Porto, masters once again of the tide. When we arrived at our designated boat ramp—a narrow cobblestone switchback set into Porto's old looming quay—António was there. I don't know how he did it, but he had backed his enormous truck all the way down to the water's edge.

Standing on deck, we cut the rigging and struggled to remove the mast. It was stuck. Really stuck—swollen, apparently, in its step. All we could do, at first, was laugh. But since we couldn't move the boat without removing the mast, we kept at it, rocking, pulling, and rocking again. It took four of us half an hour, grunting and swearing the whole time, but we finally uprooted that stubborn piece of spruce. The moment it came loose we let out a cheer, and hoisted it above our heads like a trophy of war, a golden lance in the setting sun.

Then, as a school of silver minnows darted about our ankles, we strapped on those damned dollies one last time. The rough cobblestones would surely bust a few of their wheels, but what did that matter now? With António's electric winch and a dozen helping hands, the *Cork Boat* was soon lumbering out of the water, up and onto the truck's flatbed, dripping and dangling seaweed from its long voyage down the Douro. Bobbing in the nearby shallows, a lone cork suddenly caught my eye. I could see it was one of our own—a Ribbit! In hauling out the boat, we must have finally snagged some netting. Amazingly, it was the only cork we had lost during the entire odyssey.

Wistful, I turned away, and walked up the ramp. And so the journey of the *Cork Boat* ended, just as it began—a single cork, afloat in my imagination.

Epilogue

The *Cork Boat* remains in Portugal. Back in Ann Arbor, my parents are still saving corks, and the wooden bowl is filling up again. But Garth says that, for our next project, we ought to build a rocket ship out of bottle caps. I've always wanted to go to the moon.

Acknowledgments

The *Cork Boat* was a team effort, beginning with my parents, Lana and Henry Pollack, whose love, support, and faith in me have made all the difference in my life.

I am also indebted to my friend Garth Goldstein. His creativity, talent, and enthusiasm were all instrumental—not just in building the boat to the highest aesthetic and functional standards, but in making our long row down the Douro such a grand adventure. Perhaps even more important, he taught me that fun and friendship can flourish despite sharp conflict, a lesson I will always remember. Forty years from now, when we are both old men sitting in Michigan Stadium cheering the Wolverines on to yet another national championship, I am sure we will still be reminiscing about our voyage together with undiminished zeal.

I am also immeasurably grateful to those many volunteers who worked so hard and in such good cheer sorting through nearly a third of a million corks and transforming them into a beautiful and seaworthy craft. In addition to Zoë Neuberger, whose love and encouragement helped keep me going in those tough, early months of construction, several other people stand out as superstars, including Jock Friedly, Michele Rivard, Katherine Switz, Heather Hurlburt, and Andrea Felix. Harold Wilson and Joe Zelinka—neighbors across the alley—were vital supporters, too. Special thanks are also due to the Lamont Street Collective, whose members opened their garage and their home to boat and boatbuilders alike, always in the best spirit of hospitality.

This project would not have been possible, either, without the extraordinarily generous support of Jochen Michalski and his entire team at the Cork Supply Group. His faith in this idea kept us afloat, literally. Several people at the company played special roles in seeing this project through, especially Chris Sipola, Francisco Pinto, James Herwatt, Isabel Allegro, and Raquel Filipe and her staff at Global Quality Control. Of all those at the Cork Supply Group, however, I owe a special thank-you to Jorge Osório, whose enthusiasm, charm, knowledge, and can-do spirit helped the *Cork Boat* and its crew surmount every obstacle, and who showed me once again that there are great friends in this world we just haven't met yet.

Many other people, businesses, and institutions pitched in on this project as well. A partial list includes Sally Pollack, Miles Lackey, Todd Cohen, Charnan Lewis, Keegan Eisenstadt, Melitta Jakab, Phil Guire, Rachel Conway, Kim Kovach, Winter Torres, Andrew Patzman, Allison Remsen, Mike Hacker, Sarah Wilson, Bruce Yoon, Alan Kadrofske, Sarah Dufendach, Rodger Citron, Bridget Andrews, Fred Clarke, Paula Short, Mike Short, Jonathan Stivers, Kathy Gille, Doug Tanner, Maya Berry, Darrel Drobnich, Lawrence Sheets, Chris Dege, John Akers, Jeff Nussbaum, Sam Afridi, Josh Gottheimer, Jed Hakken, Maria Burke, Howard and Krystyn Moon, Darius Sivins, Andy Nyblade, Matt Gelman, Barbara Bush, Bob Michitarian, Walter Lynn, Ezra Lynn, Caleb

King, Gretchen King, Steve Robinson, Shelley Robinson, Mimi Conway, Beth Sullivan, Timothy Sullivan, Karen Pence, Erich Pfuehler, Mary Feinsinger, Adri Jarayatne, Vidhya Muthuram, Nick Anderson, Esther Schrader, Warren Brown, Sean Carroll, Charlie Chambers, Chuck Brain, Alex Keenan, Wendy Koch, and their daughter Mary, Julia Dufendach, Anna Dufendach, Liz Katkin, Rich Waryn, Michael Green, Suzanne and Skip Gwiazda, Julie Martinez, Mike Newman, Betsy Palmer, Alison Perkins, Jason Cohen, Kathy Pollack, Harry Pollack, Nicole Rothstein, Laura Schiller, David Bonior, Tomas Mezaros, Charles Harple, Tara Quinn, Dave Chapman, Inga Chapman, John Podesta, Jim Garavaglia, Barb Garavaglia, Jan "Alabama Belle" Vulevich, Tommy Croxton, Judy Croxton, Leah Gunn, Bob Gunn, Naomi Gottlieb, Ted Harrison, Marta David, Ray Brown, Cokie Roberts, Steve Roberts, Donna Shalala, Tom Hayden, Jack Veneziano, Camilla Rothwell, Nora Pouillon, Ann Marsh, Michael Brooks, Erin Martin, Salah Zarar, Julie Ford, Chris Malley, Bonnie the Elevator Operator, Peter Weber, John Monagan, Joerg Lehmann, Sabine Geul, Susanne Renner, James Miller, Terry Edmonds, Doug and Mary Kelley, Diego D'Ambrosio, Edis González, Judy and Larry Pazol, Tom and Judy Pazol, Karen Pazol, Stuart Lipkin, Lawrence Pollack, Jan Grimsley, Karl Longstreith, Marcy Heisler, Barbara Fagan-Smith, Colin Smith, Mark Weiner, Jonathan Landreth, the Library of Congress, the United States Navy, the University of Michigan, Shalom Baranes Associates, the District of Columbia Harbor Patrol, Bacon Sails, Bainbridge Aquabatten, Alamo Flag, All Ways Transportation, Kuehne & Nagel, United Parcel Service, Amtrak, Abe's Towing, the United States Postal Service, the District of Columbia Jewish Community Center, the Natural Cork

Quality Council, the Alliance Rubber Company, and the Embassy of Portugal.

Many Washington restaurants played a critical role in saving corks for the boat. Among them were Restaurant Nora, Pizzeria Paradiso, San Marco's, I Matti, Osteria Otello, Tomate, Toledo Lounge, District Chop House, Fasika's Ethiopian Restaurant, Cashion's Eat Place, Cities, Tryst, Timberlake's, Anna Maria's, Ruth's Chris Steak House, Athens Taverna, Greek Taverna, Odeon Café, Buca di Beppo, Capital Hilton, Rumors, Biddy Mulligan's, The Diner, Georgetown Seafood Grill, Big Hunt, Luna Grill, El Rincón Español, Bardia's New Orleans Café, Grill from Ipanema, Pesce, and—in Ann Arbor—Paisano's. I apologize if I have omitted other contributors, as I surely have.

Once in Portugal, many people and institutions welcomed the *Cork Boat* and helped us on our way. Olga Sousa, Sónia Rodriguez, and the team at MSG-Mensagem were vital catalysts for our tremendous reception, as well as kind guardians throughout the media storm that ensued. I am also grateful to Pedro Negrão and the Douro Azul Company, Francisco Lopes and the entire Instituto Navegabilidade do Douro, António Passos and the Garagem da Lapa, Apcor, JP Vinhos, the village of Barca de Alva, José Antonio Neto Carneiro, Luis, Su, and Diogo Reis, Miles Edlmann and the staff at Quinta do Vesuvio, Docelina Pinto and her lovely staff in Sra. da Ribeira, the staff of the Vintage House, Armando Pereira Amaral, António Silva and the entire Associaçao Amigos Abeira Douro, the Casa do Douro, the Bombeiros Voluntários de Resende, the Club Nautico in Caldas de Aregos, Quinta dos Agros, Luis Candido and the crew of the *Douro Acima,* the crew of the *José Ribeira,* Mayor José Oliveira of

Bitetos, the staff of Porto's Hotel Mercure Batalha, Stefano Marello, Adrian Bridge, Mayor Paulo Teixeira of Castelo de Paiva, Mayor Luís Filipe Menezes of Vila Nova de Gaia, Eduardo Pida and the crew of the *Rio Douro,* Gerónimo the night watchman, Filipe Freire, Manuel Fontes, and the many kind strangers who cheered us onward as we labored at the oars.

I offer special thanks, also, to the crew of my beloved vessel, the *Cork Boat.* Their muscle, spirit of adventure, and sense of humor proved equally important to our success, though not necessarily in that order. In addition to my parents and Garth, these stalwarts include Brandt Goldstein (whose friendship and counsel have made such a difference in my life), Debra Nichols, Joanie Binkow, Jennifer Balch, Curtis Runyan, Aureliano Matos, Liliana Melo, Tamar Amalia Schoenberg, and Garvin "Long Oar" Heath.

I also want to thank those who helped me as I put the story of the *Cork Boat* into words, especially Tina Bennett at Janklow & Nesbit Associates, who saw the story's potential from the outset, and Andrew Miller at Pantheon Books, who was equally enthusiastic. Others who helped make this book possible include Janice Goldklang, Altie Karper, Suzanne Williams, James Kimball, Amber Hoover, and Svetlana Katz. I am also grateful to several volunteer editors for their keen insights. Those not already mentioned in other capacities include Mara Silver (who also put in a lot of hard hours building the boat), Bill Bisanz, Barbara Kancelbaum, Kenny Weine, and Andrew Scott.

Finally, I want to acknowledge my late mentor, Bill Montalbano, a supremely talented writer and generous teacher, who urged me to write books. Many years back, he contributed a cork or two. I hope I've put them to good use.

About the Author

John Pollack was a speechwriter for President Bill Clinton. Before working at the White House, he wrote speeches on Capitol Hill and spent several years in Spain as a foreign correspondent. A dogged punster, he won the 1995 O. Henry World Pun Championships, his first and only world title. He still saves corks.

Atlantic Ocean

FRANCE

Douro River

Porto

PORTUGAL

SPAIN

Lisbon

Mediterranean Sea

Porto

Vila Nova
de Gaia

Atlantic Ocean

Leverinho

CRESTUMA DAM

Bitetos

*CARRAPATELO
DAM*

Caldas
de Aregos

Peso da Régua

Rede

*BAGAUSTE
DAM*

PORTUGAL